The Drama of Prince Arjuna

(BEING A REVALUATION OF THE CENTRAL THEME OF THE BHAGVAD GITA)

SYED MEHDI IMAM, M.A. (OXON.)
BARRISTER-AT-LAW

THE BURNER

ARJUNA : *What if my deeds fail, renunciation recede, and all my vows into ruin break ? What of the absolute failure ?*

LORD KRISHNA : *Bring all your failures to My Light; your renunciation to My Beams; your vows to Me. I am the grand Crematorium whose Radiance burns to ashes all the lapses of the Spirit. Know Arjuna that all failures are but pauses. All pauses are the steps of concealed releases. All releases are Love.*

(*THE AUTHOR*)

VERITAS VINCIT OMNIA.
Truth conquereth all things.

MOTILAL BANARSIDASS
DELHI :: VARANASI :: PATNA

©MOTILAL BANARSIDASS
Indological Publishers & Booksellers

Head Office : BUNGALOW ROAD, JAWAHAR NAGAR, DELHI-7
Branches : 1. CHOWK, VARANASI-1 (U.P.)
2. ASHOK RAJPATH PATNA-4 (BIHAR)

First Edition : Delhi 1973
Price : R MLBD
0 100.00

Printed in India

BY SHANTILAL JAIN, AT SHRI JAINENDRA PRESS, BUNGALOW ROAD, JAWAHAR NAGAR, DELHI-7 AND PUBLISHED BY SUNDARLAL JAIN, MOTILAL BANARSIDASS, BUNGALOW ROAD, JAWAHAR NAGAR, DELHI-7

DEDICATION

PERFECTION

"That is full; this is full. The full comes out of the full. Take the full from the full, the full remains."

(Isa Upanishad : Translated by Radhakrishnan)

Peace, Peace, Peace.

These pages are dedicated to the first philosopher of our age, sometime President of the Republic of India, S. RADHAKRISHNAN, whose translation of the Bhagvad Gita has inspired the composition of this "Drama of Prince Arjuna", and whose services to letters and thought will remain the abiding treasure of this generation. May his eye dwell with rich regard on this play of Sri Krishna and Arjuna !

CONTENTS

PROEM

The Magic Flute

Time cannot close the whispering of hidden notes,
Love cannot hide the breath where calm reposes,
When both have mingled where the late breeze floats
Carrying such music when the evening closes !

That music which the trembling lip blows forth,
Ministering sweet sounds through an eternal reed,
O flute of Krishna ! from the South and North,
From East and West the Nations pay thee heed !

Commingling harmonies of birth and death,
In one sweet thought the whole of music rings,
Through voids uncharted and the mists of breath
One wail, where all the starry cosmos sings !

How have those strains one mesh engirdled world
Caught wrapt in threads of silver music bound,
Unveiled the ghosts of Lands whose flags unfurl'd
Lie in the dawns of the Infinite round !

More swift, more subtle and more silent than
Strange sounds we hear o'er fretful Earth's domains,
Thy songs, thy flute to turn the ears of man
Towards the mystic call of thy refrains !

We hear, play on, such music brings a peace
O Heavenly Sire, with Love's impassioned touch
Close in our hearts such echoing notes as these
And let our lives be filled with joy as much !

The full brimm'd bowl of dark'ning sky spills o'er
With dawn, impell'd to rise before the sun,
Such music calls thro' night and day with pow'r
As Beauty holds when God and man are One !

***

The Ark,
Hazaribagh,
January 1,1973

Alfred Raoul Hasan Imam

INTRODUCTION

THE PLAY

ARJUNA : Warm are the streets of the Kurus ; fallen their buildings ; and desolate their homes. How by the ire of our bombs is their fair city lit !
LORD KRISHNA : O Arjuna of the gentle lid, the pity of it, the pity of it !
ARJUNA : Yet the predestined play must proceed from scene to scene and act to act till the curtains of the imperial drama fall majestical in the vestibule and the hall of the Chancellery of the Kurus !

(*THE AUTHOR*)

THE DRAMATIC APPROACH :

The object of this work is to present the central sense of the Bhagvad Gita in dramatic form. Of the many masters of exegesis, Mahatma Gandhi has expounded it as the testament of a political faith ; Vinoba Bhave as the call to social work ; Sri Aurobindo as the basis of his Integral Yoga ; Radhakrishnan in our times as the Philosophy of the ages. Interpretation has yet to discern the dramatic approach to the Gita. Is not the dialogue of the holy book the Lila of Lord Krishna ? Is not Arjuna the sport of Maya ? Is not the crisis of Kurukshetra a play ? Is not the reversal of Arjuna dramatic ? Is not the Yogic action of Lord Krishna a Catharsis ? Is not the conclusion—the liberation of Arjuna—a dramatic Finale ? The dramatic elements of the Gita cannot be ignored. The rudimentary seeds of the drama, however overlooked, are there !

THE TWO PLANES OF THE DRAMATIC ACTION OF THE GITA :

The dramatic action of the Gita is on two planes correlated and in accord of Spirit (Purusha) and Matter (Prakriti). In the Upper Sphere of action is the Supreme Will—immanent and transcendental—of the Paramatma and its manifestations the

Jiva-Atma and the Atma. In the Lower Sphere is the action of the Not-Self (Prakriti) in the fields of the Illusions.

THE ACTION OF THE PARAMATMA :

In the field of the Paramatma there is no action. Action relates only to the realms of Maya. The Paramatma wills but does not act. Its Will is action. It sets on foot its action in the field of its creatures. But it is not itself subject to the wheels of Samsara. It is therefore the Creator and the Watcher of the Shows of creation.

THE ACTION OF THE ATMA :

The Atma is a phase of the Paramatma. It is the Cosmic Oversoul present in all creatures. As it is a part of the Paramatma it does not act. Like the Paramatma it is the Spectator of Works. It has a double aspect. As the Cosmic Presence it is all-pervasive. It is not bound by the Laws of Time and Space. But as the Omnipresent Reality it is seated in the heart of every individual.

THE ACTION OF THE JIVA-ATMA :

The Jiva-Atma, the Cosmic Soul personalised, is the soul of the individual. It is the phase and part of the Paramatma and therefore cannot act. It is the Individual Soul as the Watcher of the fields of Samsara. It is not born and cannot die. But it incarnates in bodies life after life. Its corporeal vestures perish. But the Jiva cannot die.

THE ACTION OF THE NOT-SELF :

The personal self or the Not-Self is a creature of Matter or Prakriti. Its body mind and its material embodiment are Maya. The Not-Self and its fields are therefore illusory. Just because it is illusory, it can act in the realms of illusion. It is therefore the doer and not the spectator of the action. It works and cannot watch. Just because it is bound by Maya, it seeks release from the chains of illusion. Its field of action is not the field of the Will of the Paramatma, where the Real sees. Its place is in the regions of the Illusions.

THE UPPER SPHERE OF THE WILL :

The Upper Sphere is therefore the theatre of the Transcendental Will—the Paramatma, and its kindred phases the Atma and the Jiva-Atma. This is the position of the Divine Observers. As the Upper Sphere is not the sphere of the Illusions, and as all impact of action is below in the shows of Matter, the plane of the Will, although the place of the origin of all action, must be treated as the background of the drama of the Gita.

THE LOWER SPHERE OF THE NOT-SELF :

The principal action of the Gita takes place therefore in the Lower Sphere of the Not-Self. Here Arjuna is bound. Here he is freed. Here he meets in fleshly form the Avatar Lord Krishna. Here is the battleground of Kurukshetra.

THE LAWS OF THE ILLUSORY FIELDS :

In the field of Samsara, all Jivas or Monads evolving in the rounds of Maya are bound by the Cosmic Laws of the Paramatma.

THE LAW OF MAYA :

First is the Law of Maya. The Power of Maya is not the Power of the Illusions. If it were so, it would be illusory power which could not create. The Law of Maya is therefore the Power of the Paramatma to fashion finite creatures and finite creations in a world of Infinities. Maya means bounds. The Paramatma is the Lord of all the bounded Rings of Eternity. In the Gita the field of Kurukshetra is the first round of the labours of the incarnating Jivas.

THE LAW OF PERIODIC MANIFESTATIONS :

Second is the Law of the Periodic Manifestations. The Paramatma from eternity to eternity manifests and withdraws from manifestation. Each Manifestation is called a Day of Brahma. Each disappearance is a Night of Brahma. The Days and Nights are therefore the eternal Manifestations of the Paramatma. The action of Kurukshetra is staged in one Day of Brahma.

THE LAW OF THE GUNAS :

Third is the Law of the Gunas. Three Gunas or Forces bind the soul in the prison of the Illusions. First is the bondage of Darkness, Tamas, which blinds the Jiva to the Real. It destroys all sight of the truth. Second is the bondage of Desire, Rajas, which holds the Monad in the house of Maya by the active pressure of the cravings of the earth. Third is the bondage of Purity, Sattwa, which keeps the mortal in the coils of Good and Evil. But the Sattwic Force being the Force of the ascending perfection in every Monad is the arm of all the secret releases of the man. Kurukshetra is the field of the work of all the Gunas. The Guna of darkness is represented by the Kurus. The Guna of desire is represented by the blind King Dhritarashtra who looks vainly at the loss of power on the field of Kurukshetra. The Guna of purity is represented by Prince Arjuna. For he has transcended the three threads of the bondages.

THE LAW OF KARMA :

Fourth is the Law of Karma. It is the Law of requital. The good deed results in good. The bad deed results in evil. Kurukshetra is the playground of the Karma of the Kurus and the Pandavas.

THE LAW OF REBIRTH :

Fifth is the Law of the great perfecting—Rebirth. Jivas are born again and again in worlds of Maya for the perfection of experiences. By repeated incarnations they shed their imperfections. Lord Krishna himself leads the incarnating souls. In every age of material crisis is he born to re-establish Virtue. In the Kali Yuga of the Pandavas and the Kurus he takes birth for the struggle on the plains of Kurukshetra.

THE LAW OF THE RELEASES :

Sixth is the Law of Releases. Every Jiva by natural law must rise out of the mist of the Illusions. Bondage implies liberation. The releases envisaged in the Gita are manifold. The first release is by the abandonment of the fruits of work—Karma Yog. The second release is by Knowledge—Jnana Yog. The third release is by Love—Bhakti Yog. The triple releases cohere in one release—union with the Paramatma. In meditation and contemplation of the Paramatma is the beginning and the end of all the releases.

THE DRAMATIC CHARACTERS OF THE GITA :

The Gita is a drama of the Soul. The abstract conceptions of the Gita, summarised above, the Paramatma and its phases the Atma and the Jiva-Atma, and the material Self, Prakriti with its component parts, body mind and the material world of Maya, with all the governing Cosmic Laws which work within the Monad, move concretely into the characters of the Gita. Central in the dramatic situation is the figure of the Avatar Lord Krishna—the Paramatma veiled for Arjuna's eyes by the form of the flesh. Beside Him also in secret cover is Arjuna, the creature of Matter and Maya. In His primary role as friend and counsellor, He is Matter or Prakriti. The material self of Lord Krishna speaks with the material self of Prince Arjuna. In the secondary role—secret and occult—is seen in glimpses with the special sight of the Supernal, Lord Krishna, the Absolute. In the second aspect He is sensed as the Real. As the Real He is the Jiva-Atma, the Atma, and the Paramatma. The Paramatma is the secret Evolver. It therefore works in the field of Kurukshetra. Kurukshetra is the field of Arjuna's bondages ; the field of his duties ; the field of his triumphs; and the field of his releases. Out of the clash of arms in Samsara spring all the characters of the Holy Book—Sri Krishna, the hidden Lord of all creation, Arjuna and the hosts of the Pandavas, symbols of the Forces of Righteousness, Prince Duryodhana and the Kurus, the badge of the black brotherhood of darkness, Samjaya the subjective eye of unillumined reason, and Dhritarashtra the sightless lid of Samsara.

THE EXTERNAL ACTION OF THE GITA :

The external action of the Gita lies largely outside the pages of this sacred Scripture. The Gita is an episode of the wars of the Mahabharatas. In the famous Epic the main story of the Pandavas and the Kurus has been told. Dhritarashtra, the head of the line of the Kurus, had been crowned as the sovereign of the common House of the Pandavas and the Kurus. His sceptre stood undisputed till by reason of his blindness his kingdom passed under the customary Laws of the State to King Pandu. The coronation of Pandu created a fission in the united House of the Pandavas and the Kurus. Prince Duryodhana son of Dhritarashtra, leader of the Kurus line, raised the Kuru faction to seize the crown of Pandu. Prince Arjuna of the line of Pandu resisted with all the Pandavas the aggression without the warrant of law. The armies of the two factions met on the field of Kurukshetra to determine by arms the right of the succession to the throne of Pandu.

THE INTERNAL ACTION OF THE GITA :

The Gita is a spiritual drama. The episode of the Mahabharata taken at the point of the crisis of arms lies on the fringe of this play. The internal action of the Gita is centred on the spiritual action initiated by Lord Krishna upon the soul of Prince Arjuna. For Arjuna Kurukshetra is not only a field of action. It is rather a field of choice. The principal struggle is not in the outer plane of the battle but in the inner plane of the psyche.

THE DRAMATIC DEFECT OF ARJUNA :

The main action of the Gita springs from the dramatic defect of Prince Arjuna. His eyes are closed to the Real. He renounces the duties of battle because he does not perceive the Light of Lord Krishna. He will not fight his kinsmen because he will not slay.

THE DRAMATIC ACTION OF THE GITA :

The dramatic action of Lord Krishna proceeds to a spiritual solution. Partly by the exposition of his Holy Wisdom—the subtle annunciation of the principles of the triple Yogas of Work, Knowledge, and Love—and partly by the occult play of his eyes Lord Krishna woos and wins his reluctant votary summoning him as his consecrate warrior to the field of Kurukshetra.

THE DRAMATIC CRISIS OF THE GITA :

The secret action of the Yogas leads to the spiritual crisis of Prince Arjuna on the battleground of Kurukshetra. Should he leave his kingdom to the Kurus ? Should he renounce the call to arms ? Should he retire ? Or should he do as he is bidden by Lord Krishna—perform his work on Kurukshetra's field as sacrifice and prayer for the Supreme ? The voice of Dharma or duty emergent from the lips of the covert Paramatma determines the issue. The crisis is closed by the will of Lord Krishna. The debate of words yield to the Way of deeds. Arjuna's work proceeds without the search of the fruits of work.

THE DRAMATIC REVERSAL OF THE GITA :

The dramatic reversal of the Gita is spiritual. What collapses is not Arjuna but the illusory field of Arjuna. Lord Krishna the Real is at work in the realms of the Unreal. He strikes not his disciple but the delusions which hold the eyes of his votary. The triple Yogas cleanse the lids of Arjuna. The shadows of Samsara vanish. With free sight the Prince perceives the Atma—the true Self of man. In the reversal, the Not-Self and its material appertainances are destroyed.

THE DRAMATIC FINALE :

The dramatic finale of the Gita is the Catharsis or Purification of the passions. The goal and end is Liberation or Mukti. The action of the Yogas is the Lila or Play of Lord Krishna. The disenchantment on the field of Kurukshetra is the sport or Maya of the Paramatma. The battle of Kurukshetra is the field of the purgation of the Prince. By the performance of his duties he obtains the release. He becomes the Jiva-Mukti. His salvation is total emancipation in the life of the body.

TRAGIC PITY AND TRAGIC TERROR :

The tragic pity and the tragic terror haunt the pages of the Gita. Dramatic compassion drenches the eyes of Arjuna as he views the slaughter of the house of the Pandavas and the Kurus. Dramatic terror fills his gaze upon the form of Kali the destroyer. The dramatic fear rises to its height in his vision of the Paramatma.

THE INGREDIENTS OF DRAMA :

Thus the ingredients of drama—dramatic defect, dramatic action, dramatic crisis, dramatic reversal, and dramatic Catharsis of Liberation—exist in the Gita. From these germs is to be formulated the play of Lord Krishna and Prince Arjuna.

THE PRESENT DRAMA :

The present drama of Lord Krishna and his disciple which follows upon this introduction falls into three sections—Prologue, Act I and its correlated eighteen scenes, and the Epilogue.

PROLOGUE :

The Prologue is spoken by a figure dressed as Father Time. He is the Spirit of the Ages who reaps the harvests of the Eternities. He connects the tale of the Mahabharata with the Episode of the Gita. With a dramatic gesture he points to the Battlefield of Kurukshetra.

ACT I :

Act I contains the main action of the Gita. It consists of eighteen scenes. Each scene reproduces the substance of the eighteen chapters of the Gita.

Scene I opens with the blind King Dhritarashtra and his minister Samjaya surveying from the hill of Kurukshetra the battle of the Kurus and the Pandavas now imminent upon the plains. The war of the Mahabharata is however modernised for this generation which is conversant with bombs, planes, and artillery fire. The essential substance of the first scene of the Gita is maintained.

Scene II deals with the distress of Arjuna and the subtle discourses of Lord Krishna upon the triple Yogas which recall the Prince to the war.

In Scene III Lord Krishna expounds the essence of the path of Works, Knowledge, and Love which purge the soul of Arjuna for the battle of Kurukshetra.

In Scene IV Lord Krishna explains the mystery of Yogic Knowledge, Yogic work, and Yogic action which purify the duties of the Prince.

In Scene V Lord Krishna answers the query of Arjuna. He points out that performance of works and the renunciation of works are not oppositions but the complementary paths to the fulfilment of his duties.

In Scene VI Lord Krishna declares the meditative processes of trance and Samadhi as the active assistants of the Yogic Realisation.

In Scene VII Lord Krishna affirms Yogic Realisation as a Way for the purification of duties.

In Scene VIII Lord Krishna shows the Mystery of Brahma which cleanses the mind of Prince Arjuna for the right performance of his duties.

In Scene IX Lord Krishna reveals the secrets of Raj Yoga which sets Arjuna on the path of his royal duties.

In Scene X Lord Krishna shows the Prince the Supernal Manifestations of the Paramatma.

In Scene XI the climaxing scene of the Gita—Lord Krishna manifests before the Prince the Absolute Form of the Divine. In the Paramatmic Vision Arjuna sees the shape of Kali and the fall of the Kurus in the resounding defeat of evil on the field of the coming battle of Kurukshetra.

In Scene XII Lord Krishna states the principles of Bhakti Yoga manifest in the love worship and sacrifice of the devotee.

In Scene XIII Lord Krishna propounds the philosophy of the Not-Self in the field of Samsara, with the Atma as the Watcher, and the Paramatma beyond all the regions of the Illusions.

In Scene XIV Lord Krishna explains the triple strands of the Not-Self which pin the soul in the cycles of Samsara.

In Scene XV Lord Krishna shows the Paramatma as the Supreme Spirit transcending the mutable and the immutable Manifestations.

In Scene XVI Lord Krishna points to the two paths of the Divine and the Undivine. The first is the path of the sons of wisdom on the ascending arc to God. The second is the path of the sons of folly on the descending arc to hell.

In Scene XVII Lord Krishna tells of the threefold faiths of Tamas, Rajas and Sattwa, and the relationship of such faiths to Scripture, Worship, Sacrifice, Austerities, and Charities.

In Scene XVIII Lord Krishna closes the Gita with the exposition of the integral release by all the paths to God.

EPILOGUE :

This drama ends with the speech of the Epilogue who gives utterance to the Abstract Philosophy of the Gita.

THE MESSAGE :

Realise the Gita. Rich are its releases and sweet the wisdom of Lord Krishna's lip !

AUM

PROLOGUE

The Play's the thing
Wherein I 'll catch the conscience of the King

HAMLET : ACT II : SCENE II

(*The Prologue dressed as Father Time appears with a scythe from the mists of Maya. In a serene voice he outlines the background of the plot of the Bhagvad Gita*).

Prologue : I am the Prologue of this play. My name is Time. In my hand is a Scythe. With it I mow all the cornfields of the Ages. Their seeds I sow again and again in new furrows. Their crop I hoard in the Barn of My ancient Memories. From the Storehouse of My Reminiscences I draw here one tale myth or truth—from the holy wars of the MAHABHARATA. Briefly hear the story of the Bhagvad Gita. Once upon a time in the age of Kali Yuga, a fair kingdom lay by the sacred banks of the Jamuna. Of those realms the first crowned head was Dhritarashtra, father of Prince Duryodhana and the Kuru clan. He did not reign long. Bereaved of eyes, his coronet was forfeit to Pandu, who was enthroned by the ceremonies of the law as the sole sovereign overriding the children of Dhritarashtra. Thus the imperial house of the Kauravas was split into two. The children of King Pandu, Arjuna and his brothers, the royal seed of the line of the Pandavas—were rivalled by the sons of Dhritarashtra. The former were called the House of the Pandavas; the latter the House of the Kurus. Though of one womb and one house, the twin factions moved to war. The first—the aggregate of the Forces of virtue—assembled under the flag of Prince Arjuna and his counsellor in fleshly guise Lord Krishna. The second—the black brotherhood of evil—banded under the shadow of Prince Duryodhana and his kinsmen and cousins of Prince Arjuna. Now look to the play. Kurukshetra's holy field will decide today the issue of the crown of Dhritarashtra. (Materialising the scene) Here come, look you, the reconnoitrers the blind King Dhritarashtra and his faithful minister Samjaya sniffing the war. There, please look, is the river. Can't you see the armies of the Kurus and the Pandavas on either Bank ! Now turn this way (Showing Arjuna). There is my Lord Arjuna. How he sits with despondent lid. Can't you see his arms laid on the ground ? Don't mistake the man, please. The Prince is a soldier. Wait. He will fight all right. Now have a good peep. Just mark who comes behind him. Do look. There stalks in holy armour my Lord Krishna. Soon will his high dialogues of the Yogas restore the calm and courage of Prince Arjuna. (Hearing a sound) What's all this pother about ? Well, let the bombs fall. This is war, you know (Whispering to the Powers of Maya). Now, Elves, be still. (Turning to the audience in a voice of rising dignity) Let us to the spectacle of these high actions go. (Evoking scenes of Maya) By My magic of Maya, O curtains rise ! On Kurukshetra's embattled floor, behold Samsara's holy show ! (Pointing to the mists of materialised Maya) My noble Lords, THE BATTLEFIELD !

(The battlefield of Kurukshetra suddenly materialises from the mists. By degrees the lights of Maya fade. The Apparition of the Prologue then rapidly dissolves into air).

CHARACTERS

DHRITARASHTRA	THE BLIND KING OF THE KURUS
SAMJAYA	HIS COUNSELLOR
DURYODHANA	THE PRINCE OF THE KURUS
ARJUNA	THE PRINCE OF THE PANDAVAS
LORD KRISHNA	COUNSELLOR OF ARJUNA
MINOR CHARACTERS	GUARDS, COURIERS, DELEGATES ETC.

ACT I

SCENE I

THE PAUSE BEFORE THE BATTLE

(*The scene opens brilliantly at midday. The air is tense. The blind King Dhritarashtra is climbing the hill held by Samjaya. The battlefield lies below steeped in sunlight. The armies of the Pandavas and the Kurus are deploying on the plains. The blind King climbs the hill of Kurukshetra*).

Dhritarashtra (Groping) : O eyes !

Samjaya (Picking him up) : My Lord, you stumble !

Dhritarashtra : Can sightless orbs see ?

Samjaya : Rest, my Lord.

Dhritarashtra (Struggling) : Yet a little further—

Samjaya : Then hold my hand—

Dhritarashtra : But the soil slips. O precious sight, why wast thou to this tender lid confined ? Why am I bereaved of the light of Kurukshetra's field ?

Samjaya : My gentle Lord, pause.

Dhritarashtra : Have we reached the summit ?

Samjaya : Yes.

Dhritarashtra : Where are we ?

Samjaya : On the brow of Kurukshetra's hill.

Dhritarashtra (Hearing the sound of running water) : What purls there ?

Samjaya : The rill of Kurukshetra's wooded hill.

Dhritarashtra : Ah ! the smell of woods and the sound of streams—

Samjaya (Continuing to soothe) : Which to such sweet dispositions as yours are ministers of beauty—

Dhritarashtra : Where is beauty here ?

Samjaya : Does not the melody of birds in these lovely dales soften the lids of affliction ?

Dhritarashtra : Soon you will hear other sounds, Samjaya.

Samjaya : Is my Lord ill ?

Dhritarashtra : I but predict !

Samjaya : I do not know what you mean.

Dhritarashtra : My eyes are dim, but my scent is keen !

Samjaya : I understand not.

Dhritarashtra (Smelling war) : I smell what you cannot smell !

Samjaya (Trying to comfort) : My Lord, the sweet scent of the sylvan scenes !

Dhritarashtra : That's not the scent I scent.

Samjaya : What scent then ?

Dhritarashtra (Ruefully) : I smell Sulphur !

Samjaya (Still comforting) : The air here is sweet—

Dhritarashtra (Sharply contradicting) : The air here is sick.

Samjaya : Sick with what ?

Dhritarashtra : Sick with the sad shadows of the most inglorious war.

Samjaya (Finding himself discovered) : My Lord, you see !

Dhritarashtra : Yes, but not with the eyes of illusion. What is moving upon the plains below ?

Samjaya (Hiding) : Nothing.

Dhritarashtra (Sternly) : Hide nothing from me. For nothing from secret lid is hid. Speak plainly. Have they come to grip in battle ?

Samjaya (Still concealing) : No ! You do surely err, my Lord.

Dhritarashtra (Reproving) : You do surely lie, Samjaya.

Samjaya (Apologizing) : Your royal lips, I cannot disobey.

Dhritarashtra (Angry) : Obey or from this hill depart.

Samjaya (Obeying) : My Lord, I report.

Dhritarashtra (Stiffly) : Conceal nothing. What do you see ?

Samjaya : The World-War of the Mahabharata is afoot.

Dhritarashtra : That's nearer the truth. Go on—Speak faster.

Samjaya : The armies of the Kurus and the Pandavas are all hurrying to the river banks—

Dhritarashtra : Who are on the right bank ?

Samjaya : The Kurus.

Dhritarashtra : And the left bank ?

Samjaya : The Pandavas.

Dhritarashtra : What are they doing ?

Samjaya : Bridging the river.

Dhritarashtra : With the pontoons ?

Samjaya : The bridges sway on both sides of the river.

Dhritarashtra : Who are the warriors of the Kurus you see ?

Samjaya : Prince Duryodhana, Karna, Kripa, Bhisma, I clearly discern through my field-glasses.

Dhritarashtra : Who are the Lords of the Pandavas ?

Samjaya : Of them I mark Virata, Chekitan and Kuntibhoj. In their midst is Prince Arjuna.

Dhritarashtra : Who is beside Prince Arjuna ?

Samjaya : My Lord, Krishna.

Dhritarashtra (Fearful) : In battle gear ?

Samjaya : Yes.

Dhritarashtra : What else do you see ?

Samjaya : The amassing of troops on either bank.

Dhritarashtra : The vehicles ?

Samjaya : On either side the armoured cars are cramming the roads.

Dhritarashtra : How is the air ?

Samjaya (Suppressing the truth) : The battle is imminent.

Dhritarashtra (Suspecting) : Answer. How is the air ?

Samjaya (Reluctantly revealing) : Filling with planes.

Dhritarashtra : And the ground ?

Samjaya : Swept with tanks.

Dhritarashtra : And the artillery of either army ?

Samjaya : Hid in brake and bush.

Dhritarashtra : So none for long will hold the fatal fire ?

Samjaya (Confessing realistically) : No !

Dhritarashtra : Ah ! My shut eyes see. I prophecy. Today the roll of drums will announce the fatal feud of the Kurus and the Pandavas rushing blind into the dread horror of war for the perishable fragments of my broken domains—

Samjaya (Sadly) : Worse than war is this internecine fray where brother and brother, kinsman and kinsman, slayers and slain, are caught in the feverish glare of the mouth of hell.

Dhritarashtra : Did you hear ?

Samjaya : Yes. The trump.

Dhritarashtra : Then again the sound !

Samjaya (Dramatically) : The drum. Again the drum.

Dhritarashtra : What sounds are these, Samjaya ?

Samjaya : The sounds and cymbals of ignoble war.

Dhritarashtra : Forget then the tents of peace ! Blow the fife ! Beat the drum. Of noise, flame and steel alone, speak.

Samjaya (Breaking down) : My throat is choked, I cannot speak.

Dhritarashtra : Clear the throat. Of horror and the shapes of horror speak.

Samjaya (Calming the King) : The battle is imminent but not begun.

Dhritarashtra : Do you hold out a promise, a hope ? Any parley from the side of Prince Arjuna ?

Samjaya : None.

Dhritarashtra : No white flag ?

Samjaya : No.

Dhritarashtra : No diplomatic overture ?

Samjaya : No.

Dhritarashtra (Pleading for peace) : Where is my Lord Krishna ?

Samjaya (Looking carefully through the field-glasses) : By the armoured column near Prince Arjuna's side.

Dhritarashtra : From him no gesture ?

Samjaya : No. My Lord Krishna stands ever on wisdom's height detached from the smoke of war—

Dhritarashtra : Detached ! O clamour of the hounds of hell—detached ! (Attentive) What do I hear ?

Samjaya (Concealing the air attack) : The sound of wings.

Dhritarashtra : What wings ?

Samjaya (Still hiding the attack) : They come my Lord like a drone of angry bees from the buzzing cloudlands.

Dhritarashtra (Surprised and alarmed) : Who comes ?

Samjaya (Hinting) : Is this not the Air-Age ?

Dhritarashtra : Speak clearly.

Samjaya (Revealing the danger to the King) : Very well, then hear. The bombers of the Northern command from the hidden aerodromes of the Pandavas freighted with their burden of death sweep the skies of the Kurus.

Dhritarashtra : What is our reply ?

Samjaya : More bombers and more bombs.

Dhritarashtra (With hopes shattered) : So this is the pause of Kurukshetra's field !

Samjaya (Seeing a shower of bombs falling near the King) : Pardon me, my Lord. We must move from here without delay. My Lord, my Lord, move ! (Seeing) That's a miss !

Dhritarashtra : What loud report was that ?

Samjaya : It is not safe here.

Dhritarashtra : Why do you hold back the truth.

Samjaya : What truth do I hold back ? My Lord hears.

Dhritarashtra (Sadly) : I hear and know.

Samjaya : Then into the woods immediately !

Dhritarashtra : We go.

Samjaya (Anxiously) : Quick, my Lord ! There is no more time to waste. I have responsibilities my King.

Dhritarashtra : What shrieking sound effaces the sky ?

Samjaya (Impatient for the King's safety) : No more speech ! Those are the rockets of the New Age, my Sovereign! Away to the woods then !

Dhritarashtra (Hearing the artillery fire) : What with such violence speaks yonder ? What din is that ?

Samjaya : The artillery of the Pandavas flaming from a thousand throats of thunder. (Overcome by anxiety) My Lord must obey me.

Dhritarashtra (Evoking pity and terror) : I am old and blind. How can I move, good Samjaya ?

Samjaya (Carrying the King) : Into the woods without delay.

Dhritarashtra (Lifted by Samjaya) : Into the woods we move !

(*Exeunt Dhritarashtra and Samjaya*)

SCENE II

THE DISTRESS OF PRINCE ARJUNA

(*Prince Arjuna sitting on the wayside watching his troops pass in column after column broods on the folly of war when Lord Krishna gently taps him on the shoulder awakening him from his reverie*).

Lord Krishna : Sweet Prince, how fares the battle ?

Arjuna : Well, my Lord, well.

Lord Krishna : Wherefore this silence ?

Arjuna : Nothing my Lord nothing.

Lord Krishna (Perceiving) : What melancholy broods beneath your suppressed lids ?

Arjuna (Opening up) : My Lord reads the secret thoughts of men.

Lord Krishna : Valiant Prince, you are sick of heart ?

Arjuna (Confessing) : Yes.

Lord Krishna (Going deeper) : And feint with tears ?

Arjuna : Yes.

Lord Krishna : Affrighted by war's alarms ?

Arjuna : No.

Lord Krishna : Then why do your arms lie forsaken in the field of Kurukshetra ?

Arjuna : I am a Prince of a house of warriors. I fear not the wounds or noise of war.

Lord Krishna : Then why do you abandon the field of duty ?

Arjuna : Shall I release the truth ?

Lord Krishna : Do. Give tongue to all Samsara's shows of fears.

Arjuna : My Lord, I will not slay my kinsmen. Here before me pass not foes, but friends, sires, grandsires, cousins, brothers, teachers and students of the Vedic lore, men whom I have loved, priests whom I have adored lighting the taper on your holy shrine. What brutality commends their death ?

Lord Krishna : Dharma and duty commend their death. All the Kurus are deep-dyed in guilt. They must be destroyed. Or else the roots of evil will spread and devouring make a wilderness of this fair land of the Pandavas.

Arjuna : War is folly, my Lord. The houses of the prosperous it brings to low estate. The victor and the victim both perish.

Lord Krishna : Not all wars are folly. To abandon the struggle against evil is folly worse than war. To repudiate duty brings the vaster ruin. Oppose aggression. Strive in arms against the wrong-doers of the House of the Kurus.

Arjuna (Protesting) : Perish the guilty by their guilt, my Lord! I will not slay. Rather let me bare my breast to their wounds than wound. I will not kill my kinsmen. I will not stain my conscience with their wrongs. Desires have I none. Kingdoms I do not seek. Why should I kill, my Lord?

Lord Krishna (Looking severe) : With patience, Arjuna, listen to My Wisdom.

Arjuna (Humbly) : With most patient ears I hear my Lord.

Lord Krishna (Beginning to teach) : Learn first of the nature of My Yogic Action with which I purify my seekers.

Arjuna : What is Yogic Action? Declare, my Lord.

Lord Krishna : Yogic Action is the harmony of all actions.

Arjuna : What are its characteristics?

Lord Krishna : Detachment and Balance.

Arjuna : What proceeds from detachment?

Lord Krishna : The unclouded mind free of the shows of Samsara.

Arjuna : What does the detached judgment see?

Lord Krishna : The truth in part or whole.

Arjuna : What is Balance?

Lord Krishna : Physical, mental and spiritual equilibrium.

Arjuna : What from Balance proceeds?

Lord Krishna : The Spirit's call to holy deeds.

Arjuna : Is the balanced Yogi bound by evil?

Lord Krishna : No.

Arjuna : Is he bound by good?

Lord Krishna : No.

Arjuna : So the true action of Yoga transcends the pair of opposites.

Lord Krishna : Yes.

Arjuna : Because it is the action of the Harmonies?

Lord Krishna : Yes.

Arjuna : Is the action of Harmony free of the illusions ?

Lord Krishna : Yes, because it is the action of the Divine.

Arjuna : Then the detached and balanced Yogi is the agent of the action and not the doer of the act ?

Lord Krishna : Yes, What acts in the works of the detached and balanced Yogi.

Arjuna : The Divine action of the harmonies.

Lord Krishna : Who is the Lord of the action of the harmonies ?

Arjuna : God.

Lord Krishna : Therefore the action of the harmonies is liberate of Maya.

Arjuna : Yes.

Lord Krishna : What is the boundless action ?

Arjuna : The action of the harmonies of the Divine. What from such detachment and balance springs ?

Lord Krishna : Freedom.

Arjuna : Freedom from what ?

Lord Krishna : Freedom from the delusions of Samsara—

Arjuna : For the Divine action is free of Maya—

Lord Krishna : Because the Divine is Maya's Lord.

Arjuna : The free action is not bound by the shows of good or evil ?

Lord Krishna : No. For it transcends the pair of opposites.

Arjuna : What is free action ?

Lord Krishna : The Divine action of harmony.

Arjuna : What is bounded action ?

Lord Krishna : The undivine action of inharmony.

Arjuna : What is evil ?

Lord Krishna : Inharmony.

Arjuna : How is evil adjusted ? How are wrongs undone ?

Lord Krishna : By the action of the Divine Harmony which is embodied in the Law Karma.

Arjuna : What is Karma ?

Lord Krishna : Karma is the Universal Law of action and reaction.

Arjuna : The return of deeds for deeds, wrong for wrong, death for death, violence for violence ?

Lord Krishna : Yes.

Arjuna : Who is the creator of Karma ?

Lord Krishna : Man.

Arjuna : Who is the destructive agent of Karma?

Lord Krishna : Man. Does the violence of the Kurus to the House of the Pandavas merit violence?

Arjuna (Recovering his confidence) : My Lord, it merits violence and war.

Lord Krishna : And who should be the agent of correction?

Arjuna (Understanding) : I the head of the House of the Pandavas.

Lord Krishna : Then why do you linger and lurch?

Arjuna (Rising in courage) : Arm my hands with weapons. For I fight.

Lord Krishna : No tools are necessary for the fructification of the action of God. For in God will and not action works. I say and it is. Do you wish to see?

Arjuna : Yes.

Lord Krishna : Well, what do you behold in My supernal Light?

Arjuna (Seeing surprised) : My Lord the Kurus are slain and dead.

Lord Krishna : Slain by whom?

Arjuna : By you the Lord of Karma.

Lord Krishna : Are your hands red with the blood of the Kurus?

Arjuna : No.

Lord Krishna : For the deeds are mine and not yours.

Arjuna : The agent is not the doer—

Lord Krishna : And therefore from the action takes no taint.

Arjuna : Karma kills and not I.

Lord Krishna : Raise your gaze once more to My Light. What do you see?

Arjuna (Perceiving in trance) : My Lord the Kurus are not slain but live—

Lord Krishna : Live to be reborn for deaths afresh—

Arjuna : For the hidden seeds of Karma ripen from life to life with the heavy harvests of pain.

Lord Krishna : Hear then My lordly wisdom.

Arjuna : O sovereign Truth, speak!

Lord Krishna : The wise grieve neither for the dead nor for the living. For he that thinks he slays, knows Me not. He that thinks he is slain, knows Me not. The slayer and the slain are the forms of Maya—this vast illusion that I make. Be not entangled in the meshes of the senses, Arjuna. Nothing dies. All that is, is for ever. Beginnings and endings are the counterfeits of Mind. Nothing begins and nothing ends. All Samsara's dominions are false and fleeting. But as infancy, youth and eld come to all mortality, so the incarnating Jiva from age to age, like the snake it skins, puts off or on bodies new of Spirits old, as temporal tenements of the flesh. Many times have you been born. Many times have you died. Many times will you be born. Many times will you die. The immortal Jiva fears not death. For the Jiva cannot die. Weapons cannot cleave it. Water cannot drown it. Fire cannot consume it. Winds cannot wither it. The immortal essence of the Jiva cannot be destroyed. But as to the mutable forms which clothe the Jiva, they perish. Let them perish Arjuna. For the transient garments of the soul abide but a moment in the fleeting flux of Maya.

Arjuna : Tell me Lord what is the immortal Self and what is the mortal body ? What is the substance ? What is the Shadow ? What is Atma and what is not Atma ?

Lord Krishna : The immortal Self is the Atma not bound by the changing shapes of Samsara. It is man's immaterial nature which lies in subtle depths beyond the reach of Space and Time.

Arjuna : Therefore arms cannot touch it—

Lord Krishna : And fire cannot quench it.

Arjuna : It is therefore the perennial Self of man—

Lord Krishna : Indissoluble and immortal.

Arjuna : What is the Jiva-Atma ?

Lord Krishna : The Jiva-Atma is the individual manifestation of the Atma which incarnates life after life in the clothings of bodies.

Arjuna : Therefore the Atma and the Jiva-Atma are one ?

Lord Krishna : Yes.

Arjuna : And therefore the Jiva-Atma is not born and cannot die ?

Lord Krishna : Yes.

Arjuna : Only its vestures of Maya perish ?

Lord Krishna : Yes.

Arjuna : Its vestures are illusory then ?

Lord Krishna : Yes.

Arjuna : Then nothing perishes ?

Lord Krishna : No.

Arjuna : What is the nature of the Atma ?

Lord Krishna : The Atma is the Cosmic Soul.

Arjuna : What is the nature of the Jiva-Atma ?

Lord Krishna : The Jiva-Atma is the personal Soul ?

Arjuna : How are the Atma and the Jiva-Atma related to the Paramatma ?

Lord Krishna : The Jiva-Atma and the Atma, are the manifesting parts of the Paramatma.

Arjuna : Who is the Supreme ?

Lord Krishna : The Paramatma.

Arjuna (Comprehending the whole) : Then the Jiva-Atma, the Atma and the Paramatma are one ?

Lord Krishna : Yes.

Arjuna : What are not the Atma ?

Lord Krishna : Body and Mind.

Arjuna : What are Body and Mind ?

Lord Krishna : The shadows of Samsara.

Arjuna : What causes the shadows of Samsara ?

Lord Krishna : The Not-Self.

Arjuna : What is the Not-Self ?

Lord Krishna : Man's material nature in Space and Time.

Arjuna : What die ?

Lord Krishna : The mind and bodies of the Not-Self.

Arjuna : What is re-born ?

Lord Krishna : The Not-Self.

Arjuna : What are not re-born ?

Lord Krishna : The Atma and the Jiva-Atma.

Arjuna : Is the Not-Self a principle ?

Lord Krishna : No. The Not-Self is unreal.

Arjuna : What are the real ?

Lord Krishna : The Jiva-Atma, the Atma and the Paramatma.

Arjuna : Then nothing is born and nothing dies ?

Lord Krishna : Birth and death are the blinds of Maya.

Arjuna (Summarising) : Shall we then say that the dual nature of man is composed of the Self which is immortal and the Not-Self which is transitory and fictitious ?

Lord Krishna : Yes.

Arjuna : Shall we call the Self of man the Jiva-Atma ? For the Self of man is individualised ?

Lord Krishna : Yes.

Arjuna : Shall we say that the Self of the Universe is the Atma impersonal and cosmic ?

Lord Krishna : Yes.

Arjuna : Shall we say that the impersonal Atma and the personal Jiva form the collective category and conception of Paramatma ?

Lord Krishna : Yes.

Arjuna : The Paramatma is the Absolute unconditioned consciousness ?

Lord Krishna : Yes.

Arjuna : And the Jivas of men are the revealed parts of the Absolute ?

Lord Krishna : Yes.

Arjuna (Now realising the truth) : Then how can the Jiva-Atma die ?

Lord Krishna : It cannot die. Arjuna it cannot die.

Arjuna : What dies ?

Lord Krishna : Illusion.

Arjuna : What is illusion ?

Lord Krishna : The dream-state of the Jiva.

Arjuna : When my eyes are of the dream-state dissolved ?

Lord Krishna : Then you live in eternal duration beyond the bournes of Maya.

Arjuna : For my real nature is that of the Paramatma ?

Lord Krishna : Yes. Now answer My question with care. If your real nature is that of the Paramatma, who in battle slays ?

Arjuna : I know not.

Lord Krishna : Who is in battle slain ?

Arjuna : I know not.

Lord Krishna : For what do you grieve ?

Arjuna : I know not.

Lord Krishna : Why did you refuse to slay ?

Arjuna : I know not.

Lord Krishna : Why do you shed this vast tear on Kurukshetra's field ?

Arjuna (In tears) : Because I am illusion-bound.

Lord Krishna : Because you see not in Nescience's unholy dusk ?

Arjuna : Yes. Help, Lord (Crying Piteously).

Lord Krishna (Graciously) : Soon by My Yogas will I open wide your lids.

Arjuna : Show me the perfect action of your Yogas.

Lord Krishna (Continuing his teaching) : In the perfect action of My Yogas, my disciples are the channel of My Will. They do not act. They do not will. Look at the lilies of the dale ? Do they act ? Do they will ? Yet see how they grow. Passive are My perfect Yogis to the flow of My Force Divine.

Arjuna : Do the perfect Yogis seek the fruits of action ?

Lord Krishna : No. They have no desires.

Arjuna : What makes imperfect action ?

Lord Krishna : The craving for the fruits of action.

Arjuna : What makes the action perfect ?

Lord Krishna : The relinquishment of the fruits of action.

Arjuna : How do the perfect Yogis act ?

Lord Krishna : They act for Me without the fruits of action.

Arjuna : What do they seek in action ?

Lord Krishna : Me.

Arjuna: How should I act on Kurukshetra's sacred plains ?

Lord Krishna : Act without desire. Seek not the fruit of victories. Seek Me in the urgence of your royal duties. Shirk not the cause of noble war for the Right. Action is your royal call. Reward is not your concern !

Arjuna : One word more. Tell me of the perfect recluse. Does he sit ? Does he move ? Is he silent ?

Lord Krishna : Have you not seen a rock by a lonely shore beaten by the angry seas in perfect poise unshaken ?

Arjuna : Yes.

Lord Krishna : Does the rock move when the froth flows or the wild waves break or the wet foam strikes ?

Arjuna : No.

Lord Krishna : Does the rock stir when the sea-surf ebbs?

Arjuna : No.

Lord Krishna : For the rock is immune from the blows of the main. So My perfect recluse is immune from the shocks of Samsara.

Arjuna : Whence proceeds the immunity of the Sages?

Lord Krishna : From Me. I am their shield and arm protective.

Arjuna : How do you draw all your recluses to your Lights?

Lord Krishna : By the guided Lights of Contemplation, Work, and Adoration. My Rishis come by many ways to Me. Some by mute streams live moveless absorbed in Me. Still is their tongue. Yet they act. For invisible is their work in realms invisible. Others move and speak in forest or hamlet teaching or talking. Their work is in the material domains of Samsara. Others renounce the solitudes. They work for Me in God's holy vineyard. All My Yogis meditate, work or adore. None cherish the fruits of deeds. None nourish the desires. Untouched by action, tranquil joyous and free, they dwell in the calms of the Everlasting.

Arjuna : Let me so dwell and so act. To Kurukshetra's holy work I go. For now I KNOW.

(*Arjuna prepares to move into battle. Lord Krishna's mission is done. He retires*).

SCENE III

THE YOGA OF WORK

(*On the second day of the battle in a pause of the artillery fire Arjuna concealed in the neighbourhood of a forest is immersed in thought when Lord Krishna spies him*).

Lord Krishna : Good morrow, Prince !

Arjuna : Good morrow, Master and Guide !

Lord Krishna : What burden lies upon your countenance serene ?

Arjuna : A question my Lord. I am perplexed.

Lord Krishna : Speak.

Arjuna : Sometimes you praise Work and sometimes you laud Knowledge. Which is the higher path ?

Lord Krishna : No path is higher and no path is lower. Both paths are complementary. Both paths blend.

Arjuna : I do not understand.

Lord Krishna : Can the soul be freed from Maya without the knowledge of Maya ?

Arjuna : No.

Lord Krishna : What does Knowledge do ?

Arjuna : It liberates the lids of delusion.

Lord Krishna : How does ignorance go ?

Arjuna : By Knowledge.

Lord Krishna : Then Knowledge is a form of release ?

Arjuna : Yes.

Lord Krishna : What does consecrate Work do ?

Arjuna : It emancipates the soul from the hold of Maya.

Lord Krishna : Then work is also a form of release ?

Arjuna : Yes.

Lord Krishna : If Knowledge and Work are both releases, are they not complementary forms of liberation ?

Arjuna : Yes.

Lord Krishna : Then why do you put in opposition the Way of Knowledge and the Way of Work ?

Arjuna : The path of Knowledge and the path of Work are harmonies.

Lord Krishna : Their opposition then does not subsist ?

Arjuna : No.

Lord Krishna : Can Knowledge exist without Work ?

Arjuna : No.

Lord Krishna : Can Work exist without Knowledge ?

Arjuna : No.

Lord Krishna : Then the path of Knowledge and the path of Work do not divide ?

Arjuna : No.

Lord Krishna : Knowledge and Work are the inseparable companions on the way of Realisation ?

Arjuna : Yes.

Lord Krishna : Can anyone cease from thought ?

Arjuna : No.

Lord Krishna : Can anyone cease from work ?

Arjuna : No.

Lord Krishna : When one thinks that he does not think, he thinks ?

Arjuna : Yes.

Lord Krishna : For who can thinking stop ?

Arjuna : None.

Lord Krishna : When one thinks he does not act, he acts ?

Arjuna : Yes.

Lord Krishna : For who can action stop ?

Arjuna : None.

Lord Krishna : I the Paramatma need not action. Yet I act.

Arjuna : In Samsara's realms my Lord acts.

Lord Krishna : So thinking and acting are the obligatory processes of the releases ?

Arjuna : Yes. What are the releases of thought and action?

Lord Krishna : The release from thought is by right thinking.

Arjuna : What is right thinking ?

Lord Krishna : Meditation on My name. For My nature is Truth. And Truth is release.

Arjuna : What is right action ?

Lord Krishna : Action without the craving for the fruits of deeds.

Arjuna : What is wrong action?

Lord Krishna : Action impelled by greed, lust and anger.

Arjuna : What purifies thought and action ?

Lord Krishna : Sacrifice.

Arjuna : What is Sacrifices ?

Lord Krishna : The proffered gift of the votary's heart and hand.

Arjuna : What is the gift of the heart ?

Lord Krishna : Pure thought and pure Love.

Arjuna : What is the gift of the hand ?

Lord Krishna : Pure action free of desire.

Arjuna : Without Sacrifice, are not Knowledge, Works and Devotion vain ?

Lord Krishna : Yes. For the rites of Sacrifice are the purifiers of desire.

Arjuna : What thought binds ?

Lord Krishna : The thought tinged by the cravings.

Arjuna : What thought liberates ?

Lord Krishna : Thought free of the desires.

Arjuna : What action binds ?

Lord Krishna : The action of greed, lust and anger.

Arjuna : What action liberates ?

Lord Krishna : Actions free of the desires.

Arjuna : What consecrates the pure thought and the pure deed ?

Lord Krishna : Sacrifice.

Arjuna : What is the highest thought ?

Lord Krishna : Contemplation of the Paramatma.

Arjuna : What is the highest action ?

Lord Krishna : The action of My Rishis fixed upon My Work.

Arjuna : What is the work of your Rishis who do not work ?

Lord Krishna : Work on all My subtle planes in action subtle ?

Arjuna : What is your Work Lord ?

Lord Krishna : My Work is the Spirit's Will which beyond all works lies.

Arjuna : How do your work and will work in the worlds ?

Lord Krishna : By My manifestations on all the planes of life.

Arjuna : Whence comes Man's Work ?

Lord Krishna : From the wombs of Maya. Such work is not work but play.

Arjuna : What is the play ?

Lord Krishna : My creative Lila.

Arjuna : From whence comes Man's play ?

Lord Krishna : From the Lila of the Not-Self.

Arjuna : What is the purpose of the play in illusions rounds?

Lord Krishna : Release from the spells of the Not-Self.

Arjuna : When does true work begin?

Lord Krishna : When you are the instrument and I am the Worker.

Arjuna : What is duty then?

Lord Krishna : Duty in Maya's fields is the foundation of the releases.

Arjuna : What is the effect of the neglect of duty?

Lord Krishna : Rebirth for the performance of the duty not done.

Arjuna : What is the effect of duty done?

Lord Krishna : Duty done is My first release.

Arjuna : For duty is highest work and highest prayer.

Lord Krishna : Yes.

Arjuna : What mar all work?

Lord Krishna : The triple threads of the Not-Self.

Arjuna : What are the triple threads of the Not-Self?

Lord Krishna : Greed, lust and anger.

Arjuna : What does greed do?

Lord Krishna : It destroys the works of Man by the desires.

Arjuna : What does lust do?

Lord Krishna : It consumes the works of Man by the impassioned kiss.

Arjuna : What does anger do?

Lord Krishna : It obliterates the works of Man by the destruction of Reason.

Arjuna : Where do the works of greed, lust and anger lead?

Lord Krishna : To the three gates of the House of Hell.

Arjuna : How are the triple knots of greed, lust and anger dissolved?

Lord Krishna : By the action of My triple Yogas.

Arjuna : By pure work which cleanses?

Lord Krishna : Yes.

Arjuna : By pure knowledge which purges?

Lord Krishna : Yes.

Arjuna : By pure adoration which worships?

Lord Krishna : Yes.

Arjuna : By pure sacrifice which sanctifies ?

Lord Krishna : Yes.

Arjuna : My Lord, your jewelled wisdom has nerved my arm and clarified my eyes.

Lord Krishna : Are the lids of Samsara clearing ?

Arjuna : Yes.

Lord Krishna : See then, Arjuna, duty's course, Dharma's call and prudence's urge. Clean the House of the Kurus. To battle go !

Arjuna (*Bowing*) : My Lord, I go.

(*Arjuna moves to the front followed by Lord Krishna*).

SCENE IV

THE YOGA OF KNOWLEDGE

(*On the third day of the battle the Kurus have retreated in confusion before the advancing armies of the Pandavas. In a fir forest Arjuna is contemplating the teaching of Lord Krishna. The silence is broken by the poignant query of the Guru*).

Lord Krishna : What thought stirs your mind in the noonday ?

Arjuna : I was contemplating the many renewals of your births.

Lord Krishna : Think you that My Yoga is new ?

Arjuna : No my Lord. The roots of your Yoga stretch into infinite time.

Lord Krishna : Though not subject to birth, from generation to generation am I born by My delusive power of Maya to teach the deep mysteries of My Yoga. First Vivaswata heard it; next Manu in wisdom rich; next Ikshwaku in Vedic lore renowned; next in linked sequences the royal line of all My Rishis knew it. But in the moving march of Time, My truths grew lustreless and dim and in the age of Kali Yuga, noble Prince, perished. So in new weeds once more I come to you, My votary and friend, to revive the esoteric Mysteries of My truth on Kurukshetra's holy mead.

Arjuna : How many times have you and I been born ?

Lord Krishna : Manifold are the renewals of your births and mine. Your former lives you remember not. My former lives I know. For whenever Righteousness is encompassed by her foes, when wickedness holds high its head in pride and power; when evil men gather in bad council to blot out all virtue; from age to age I come visible in manly shape and form, to help the Good and to root out seed and branch the deep mischief of Satanic power. Thus once more I seat on Virtue's throne Virtue. He who knows the secrets of My births and the mystery of My works surely will no more be born again but will rise from the earth into the kingdom of My Light where I reside.

Arjuna : Teach me the esoteric secrets of your Yoga. What is work ? What is actionless work ? What is Sacrifice ? What is esoteric Knowledge ?

Lord Krishna : The first work is My Work which is work without desire. The four orders of Society—the order of the priesthood, the warrior, the trader and the labourer—I ordained without desire. By that act I am not stained. For no act without desire gives taint. He who acts as I act is free of blemish. Works do not bind his changeless being. Such work then is no work. For such work is release.

Arjuna : What is work and what is no-work ?

Lord Krishna : He who works with attachments works in the field of Maya. Such works bind. Such works are delusion. Such works cannot free. But he who works without attachment or desire is not bound by works. His work is no-work. His action is actionless. Such work is worklessness.

Arjuna : Who is the real doer in action which is actionlessness ?

Lord Krishna : The Atma.

Arjuna : Who is the Atma or real Self ?

Lord Krishna : I

Arjuna : Then in actionless work the Absolute is the doer ?

Lord Krishna : Yes.

Arjuna : In work which is not actionless, who is the thinker ?

Lord Krishna : The deluded Ego.

Arjuna : What does the deluded Ego think ?

Lord Krishna : It thinks it is the doer when it is not the doer.

Arjuna : Who is the doer in work which is not actionless ?

Lord Krishna : The Not-Self.

Arjuna : The Not-Self is the deluded Ego—

Lord Krishna : Which does not exist ?

Arjuna : Yes.

Lord Krishna : The work of thc Not-Self is illusion ?

Arjuna : Yes.

Lord Krishna : Then how can the work of the Not-Self liberate ?

Arjuna : It cannot liberate.

Lord Krishna : Who is the master of the Not-Self ?

Arjuna : The Atma.

Lord Krishna : What does the Atma do ?

Arjuna : It watches the work of the Not-Self in the fields of illusion.

Lord Krishna : Is actionless action illusion ?

Arjuna : No. For it is the action of the Atma which is beyond the field of illusion.

Lord Krishna : What is actionless action ?

Arjuna : Action free of attachment performed with the knowledge that the Absolute is the doer.

Lord Krishna : What is Sacrifice Arjuna ?

Arjuna : Sacrifice is the oblation of the disciple to the Giver God.

Lord Krishna : I am the oblation. I am the Giver. I am the Gift.

Arjuna : What forms do gifts and worship take ?

Lord Krishna : Many forms. Some give their material riches; some their austerities; some their works; some their knowledge; some their worship; some their inward and outward breath; some seek the higher divinities; some search for the shadows of the Astral Fields; some embrace Me alone. Every oblation I receive with equal eye.

Arjuna : What is your highest Gift ?

Lord Krishna : My Grace which purifies all works and all actions.

Arjuna : What is the relationship of Sacrifice to Works ?

Lord Krishna : Works without Sacrifice give no release.

Arjuna : What gives release ?

Lord Krishna : Consecrate work.

Arjuna : For Sacrifice is Brahma.

Lord Krishna : Through Brahma, work becomes no work but release.

Arjuna : Then Work, Sacrifice, and Consecration, are all secret approaches to Brahma—

Lord Krishna : Portions of the paths which lead to Me.

Arjuna : What is esoteric Knowledge ?

Lord Krishna : Esoteric Knowledge is a consuming Fire.

Arjuna : What does the Fire consume ?

Lord Krishna : Works.

Arjuna : What does it cleave ?

Lord Krishna : The Knot of Nescience.

Arjuna : What does it burn ?

Lord Krishna : The fields of the Illusions.

Arjuna : What does it unveil ?

Lord Krishna : The Real.

Arjuna : What does it destroy ?

Lord Krishna : The Not-Self.

Arjuna : What does it Illumine ?

Lord Krishna : This darkened vale of tears.

Arjuna : For esoteric Knowledge is esoteric Light ?

Lord Krishna : Yes.

Arjuna : How are Work and Sacrifice related to Knowledge ?

Lord Krishna : Work, Sacrifice, and Knowledge are collaborative releases.

Arjuna : What is the goal of Knowledge ?

Lord Krishna : God.

Arjuna : How do Work, Sacrifice, and Knowledge relate to my release ?

Lord Krishna : Can you not see the shapes of your release ? Above, around, below, through all My Cheats and counterfeits and show, in all Samsara's darkened air, do I not prepare for you the rounds and roads of the Freedom to which you go ?

Arjuna : O Light of the World, give me light to see and know !

Lord Krishna : What would you see and know ?

Arjuna : What is my work in Maya's red domain ?

Lord Krishna : Righteous war on holy Kurukshetra's ensanguined terrain.

Arjuna : My Lord, do you incite to violence ?

Lord Krishna : No, Prince I incite to peace.

Arjuna : How ?

Lord Krishna : Is not holy war holy work ?

Arjuna : Yes.

Lord Krishna : Is not holy work release ?

Arjuna : Yes.

Lord Krishna : Is release peace ?

Arjuna : Yes.

Lord Krishna : What is the high work of righteous war ?

Arjuna (Shocked and surprised) : Peace !

Lord Krishna : Yes, peace ! What is retraction from righteous war ?

Arjuna : Langour and ease.

Lord Krishna : What do langour and ease conspire ?

Arjuna : War with the Atma—

Lord Krishna : Which brings not peace.

Arjuna (Juggling with words) : Then war is peace and peace is war—contradictions sweet !

Lord Krishna : Harmonies fine to the tuned ear of wisdom. How should righteous war not bring peace ? How should unrighteous tears not bring war ?

Arjuna : Then my work in Kurukshetra's field is release ?

Lord Krishna : Yes.

Arjuna : What is my oblation ?

Lord Krishna : The warrior's wound and the warrior's victory.

Arjuna : What is my Knowledge ?

Lord Krishna : The wisdom of the triple Yogas.

Arjuna : What is the spiral point of my ascent ?

Lord Krishna : I. For I am the Mystic Knowledge.

Arjuna : Esoteric Lord, who are you ? Man in the Divine ?

Lord Krishna : No, the Divine in the Man.

Arjuna (Seeking Knowledge) : Are you Name and Form ?

Lord Krishna : My Rishis know Me by many names. They call Me Jiva-Atma, Atma, Paramatma, God and Divinity unguessed. Yet vain is the Rosary of My Names. For I am nameless, formless, soulless, mindless, timeless, spaceless, the Cosmic Whole. I am the Sacrifice, the Altar and the Fire. I am the smoke. I am the Real. I am the Unreal. Arjuna, Arjuna, I am you. O wandering disciple, is not the part the whole and is not the whole the part ? Is not all identity absolute ?

Arjuna : I grip the Truth !

Lord Krishna (Predicting) : So with truth to your victories move.

Arjuna (In humility) : My duties I understand and armed with truth to battle I move.

(*Exeunt Arjuna and Lord Krishna*)

SCENE V

THE RENUNCIATION OF WORKS

(*On the fourth day of the battle with the recession of the Kurus in flight gun fire has ceased. An uneasy peace pervades the place. Arjuna is strolling on the grass at dusk meditating on the teachings of Yoga when Lord Krishna observes his puzzled look*).

Lord Krishna : Perplexed Arjuna ?

Arjuna : Yes. Your doctrines are new.

Lord Krishna : What is the problem ?

Arjuna : At one moment you praise work and at another you laud the cessation of work.

Lord Krishna : Are the two situations incompatible ?

Arjuna : Apparently.

Lord Krishna : Why ? Work with the abandonment of the fruits of action leads to what ?

Arjuna : To release and the bliss that follows release.

Lord Krishna : Cessation of work with the renunciation of the fruits of action leads to what ?

Arjuna : To release and the bliss that follows release.

Lord Krishna : Then the two paths unite ?

Arjuna : Yes.

Lord Krishna : Then work and cessation from work with attachments renounced are the complementary ways to the Absolute ?

Arjuna : Yes.

Lord Krishna : True renunciation of works and the true performance of works are not oppositions ?

Arjuna : For they are harmonies.

Lord Krishna : What is the true performance of work ?

Arjuna : Work without attachments.

Lord Krishna : Who is the doer of the work in works without attachments ?

Arjuna : The Absolute.

Lord Krishna : Who is not the doer of the work without attachments ?

Arjuna : The Not-Self.

Lord Krishna : The doer of the works without attachment is the agent and the master of his works is God ?

Arjuna : Yes.

Lord Krishna : Such works purify the passions ?

Arjuna : Yes—

Lord Krishna : Subjugate the senses and conquer the mind ?

Arjuna : Yes.

Lord Krishna : And therefore lead to the governance of body and mind—

Arjuna : Yes.

Lord Krishna : And the governance of body and mind lead to enlightenment ?

Arjuna : Yes.

Lord Krishna : And enlightenment leads to truth ?

Arjuna : Yes.

Lord Krishna : The enlightened Yogi knows that he is the instrument of the working Spirit ?

Arjuna : Yes.

Lord Krishna : He grasps that the Absolute is the Lord of all works ?

Arjuna : Yes.

Lord Krishna : He perceives that body and mind and feelings are the agencies of the Not-Self—

Arjuna : Yes.

Lord Krishna : He understands that he is not body or mind but the Atma changeless in change ?

Arjuna : Yes.

Lord Krishna : He realises that he is Atma, that all beings are Atma, and that there is nought but Atma ?

Arjuna : Yes.

Lord Krishna : In Atmic rest, what else does he see ?

Arjuna : He sees the Absolute in the part and the part in the Absolute without break or fissure.

Lord Krishna : The One Reality without a second ?

Arjuna : Yes.

Lord Krishna : The One in the many and the many in the One. What is the heart of that One Reality ?

Arjuna : The Cosmic calm of Brahma.

Lord Krishna : What are the marks of the emancipated Yogi ?

Arjuna : Serenity of mind and tranquility of the body centred on the ray of the Absolute above the sway of love or hate.

Lord Krishna : For he has passed beyond the shades of night or day.

Arjuna : You have taught me, Lord, the Yogas of Work, Knowledge, Sacrifice and Desire. What of the Yoga of Love and Devotion ?

Lord Krishna : Let me speak to you symbolically. For how should you know of Love save by symbolic hints ? Look at this slender lily a-drip with dew. Is it nourished by the rains ?

Arjuna : Yes.

Lord Krishna : Bathed by the air ?

Arjuna : Yes.

Lord Krishna : Cherished by the sun ?

Arjuna : Yes.

Lord Krishna : Drawing its nutriments from fibres and filaments rare ?

Arjuna : Yes.

Lord Krishna : If some ungentle hand cut its roots, would not its white hood droop and die ?

Arjuna : Yes.

Lord Krishna : Its leaves and petals fade ?

Arjuna : Yes.

Lord Krishna : Could the rain and the wind and the sun save it ?

Arjuna : No.

Lord Krishna : What is the root of all the Yogas ?

Arjuna : Love.

Lord Krishna : If the root of Love in all the Yogas were cleft, would Yoga survive ?

Arjuna : No.

Lord Krishna : Can the Yogi of work work without love ?

Arjuna : No.

Lord Krishna : Can the Yogi of knowledge know without love ?

Arjuna : No.

Lord Krishna : Then the Yoga of Love is the latent life behind the Yoga of Work and Knowledge ?

Arjuna : Yes.

Lord Krishna : What is the highest Love ?

Arjuna : The adoration of the Supreme.

Lord Krishna : What is the highest Yoga ?

Arjuna : The synthesis of Work, Knowledge, and Love ?

Lord Krishna : What lies in the fiery heart of the Universe ?

Arjuna : Cosmic Love.

Lord Krishna : What evolves in the silent womb of the Cosmos ?

Arjuna : Love and the dreams of love in manifold manifestation beneath the dread eye of God.

Lord Krishna : Are then Work and Knowledge not Love ?

Arjuna : Yes.

Lord Krishna : Then in battle work and know and love.

Arjuna : I will my Lord.

(*Enchanted by the discourse of Lord Krishna, Arjuna falls into a trance. Lord Krishna quietly withdraws unmarked*).

SCENE VI

THE YOGA OF MEDITATION

(*On the fifth day of the battle, Arjuna is meditating in the shrine of Kali near the front when Lord Krishna surprises him*).

Lord Krishna : Prince !

Arjuna (Surprised) : My Lord is here ?

Lord Krishna (Smiling) : I am always here.

Arjuna : I was contemplating in your temple before the battle—

Lord Krishna : What's the theme ?

Arjuna : Meditation.

Lord Krishna : What do you wish to know ?

Arjuna : What is Meditation ? How is the Meditative process connected with the path of Works and Knowledge and Devotion ?

Lord Krishna : Works, Knowledge and Devotion prepare the spirit for the higher ascents.

Arjuna : What are the higher ascents ?

Lord Krishna : The high roads to Meditation.

Arjuna : What is the peak of the ascents ?

Lord Krishna : Meditation.

Arjuna : How do works prepare the paths to Meditation ?

Lord Krishna : The renunciation of the fruits of work, sacrifice and actionless action, destroy passion, lust and anger which are the impediments of Yoga.

Arjuna : When the impediments of Yoga are removed, what follows ?

Lord Krishna : The governed mind in a governed body.

Arjuna : What does the governed mind in the governed body produce ?

Lord Krishna : The equipoise of all the Yogas.

Arjuna : What is the equipoise of the Yogas ?

Lord Krishna : Habitual detachment, balance, serenity in all circumstances of life whether of pleasure or pain.

Arjuna : The Yogic discipline of Self-Control clears the way to Meditation ?

Lord Krishna : Yes.

Arjuna : How does Knowledge prepare ?

Lord Krishna : By removing the veils of Maya.

Arjuna : What are the veils of Maya ?

Lord Krishna : The Not-Self with its coverings body and mind.

Arjuna : What lies beneath the coverings of Maya ?

Lord Krishna : The Atma.

Arjuna : What does Knowledge bring in her holy basket of preparations ?

Lord Krishna : The radiant lights of the changeless Atma concealed in the shelves of the Not-Self.

Arjuna : To what do the radiant lights of the holy Atma point ?

Lord Krishna : To the rare roads of Meditation.

Arjuna : How does Devotion prepare ?

Lord Krishna : By Love.

Arjuna : What does the lover of God give ?

Lord Krishna : All.

Arjuna : His works ?

Lord Krishna : Yes.

Arjuna : Riches of his Knowledge ?

Lord Krishna : Yes.

Arjuna : Wealth of his oblations ?

Lord Krishna : Yes.

Arjuna : Lips of his worship ?

Lord Krishna : Yes.

Arjuna : Tokens of his prayers ?

Lord Krishna : Yes.

Arjuna : What does he reserve ?

Lord Krishna : Nothing.

Arjuna : Then of all possessions is he dispossessed ?

Lord Krishna : Yes.

Arjuna : What does his dispossession bring ?

Lord Krishna : The radiant lights of the Atma hid in the meshes of the Not-Self.

Arjuna : What is the common aim of Work, Knowledge and Devotion ?

Lord Krishna : The opening in the Not-Self of the radiant light of the Atma.

Arjuna : What is the goal of the triple Yogas ?

Lord Krishna : Meditation on the Atma.

Arjuna : What is the effect of Meditation ?

Lord Krishna : Release from all the worlds of Maya.

Arjuna : What is the effect of the Meditative release ?

Lord Krishna : An awakening to the Real.

Arjuna : What is the effect of the awakening to the Real ?

Lord Krishna : The destruction of the Night of Nescience and the end of Maya's vexing dreams.

Arjuna : In the meditative state of trance what recedes ?

Lord Krishna : Works of body and mind.

Arjuna : Why ?

Lord Krishna : Body and mind are parts of the Not-Self in the bondages of the Illusions. The flames of the Atma in the meditating Yogi burn our all illusions.

Arjuna : Therefore the Fire of the Atma extinguishes all the works of body and mind ?

Lord Krishna : Yes.

Arjuna : Then body and mind are not present in the meditative trance ?

Lord Krishna : No. For all illusions have been killed.

Arjuna : What is present in the meditative drowse ?

Lord Krishna : The All pervasive Presence of the Paramatma—

Arjuna : Enfolding the realms of Samsara ?

Lord Krishna : Yes.

Arjuna : And transcending the regions of Maya ?

Lord Krishna : Yes.

Arjuna : For the Cosmic Soul is the Omnipresent Reality ?

Lord Krishna : Yes.

Arjuna : It is therefore nowhere absent.

Lord Krishna : Yes.

Arjuna : The meditative trance is therefore the trance of the All ?

Lord Krishna : Yes.

Arjuna : What are the steps of the meditative ascent to the Atma ?

Lord Krishna : By the conquest of the Lower Self.

Arjuna : How is the Lower Self conquered ?

Lord Krishna : By the firm discipline of My triple Yogas of Work, Knowledge and Devotion.

Arjuna : By works which clean, by knowledge which sees, and by love which draws?

Lord Krishna : Yes.

Arjuna : And what of the Yogi who has reached the Atmic plane?

Lord Krishna : Awake or asleep, he lives in Me. For I am he and he is I.

Arjuna : In the union of the Jiva-Atma with the Paramatma?

Lord Krishna : Yes.

Arjuna : What does he do in the Immutable plane of the Paramatma?

Lord Krishna : He watches the play of the mutable in the plane of the attachments.

Arjuna : The Shows of Samsara?

Lord Krishna : Yes.

Arjuna : What works does he do in the Atmic plane?

Lord Krishna : Subtle works in the subtle planes.

Arjuna : Works of body and mind?

Lord Krishna : No. The work of the visible has ended.

Arjuna : What is the nature of his works invisible?

Lord Krishna : The viewless works of the viewless Spirits—

Arjuna : Incomprehensible to mind and beyond cognition?

Lord Krishna : Yes. For he works in the plane of the Will.

Arjuna : His works are therefore the works of the Paramatma?

Lord Krishna : Yes. For he is the channel of the Force but not the Force.

Arjuna : What objects of Knowledge does he pursue in the Atmic Light?

Lord Krishna : Knowledge without objects, objects without form, forms without matter.

Arjuna : What does he seek in the Atmic Light?

Lord Krishna : Nothing. The search has ended. He is the Atmic Light.

Arjuna : What is his body?

Lord Krishna : The Paramatma.

Arjuna : What is his mind?

Lord Krishna : The Paramatma.

Arjuna : What is the body of the Paramatma?

Lord Krishna : All the fields of the Manifestations in the Days and Nights of Brahma.

Arjuna : What is the mind of the Paramatma ?

Lord Krishna : The creative Will of the Lila of the Paramatma.

Arjuna : How does your holy Yogi in his low descent to the dust dwell in Samsara's realms ?

Lord Krishna : Content he dwells and tranquil in the dells of the earth.

Arjuna : In forests of calm ?

Lord Krishna : Yes.

Arjuna : With the dripping rock as his roof ?

Lord Krishna : Yes.

Arjuna : Beside a murmuring brook far from the haunts of men, loved or unloved but loving, in sun and rain tranquil, troubling none and troubled by none, your yellow-robed Yogi lives in the rest of the Atma ?

Lord Krishna : Yes. Unimpassioned is his life, abstract his contemplation, impersonal his regard, few his wants. Lying on the silent grass beneath a canopy of moving stars, for him suffice the deerskin and the loin cloth and the water-pot. Moderate in eating, moderate in drinking, moderate in sleep, morning and evening, he draws the tranquil breath inward or outward, long or short, suspended or ceased, in varied postures of the body, harmonised to the Spirit' stress, with the lower mind silent and gathered up to seize in one rushing moment of bliss the rapture of the Paramatma !

Arjuna : What does he behold in the holy vision of the Paramatma ?

Lord Krishna : Worlds within worlds, silent and secret, suffused with the Life of the Paramatma—

Arjuna : In compass broad and wide ?

Lord Krishna : Yes.

Arjuna : Beyond the circumference of the heavens and the earths ?

Lord Krishna : Yes.

Arjuna : And what of mankind ?

Lord Krishna : He sees not man but the Atma in the man.

Arjuna : The Changeless Truth and not the changeable forms of Maya ?

Lord Krishna : Yes.

Arjuna : What of compassion then?

Lord Krishna : The Rays of the Atma warm My Yogi—

Arjuna : So that he loses not his kinship with the dust?

Lord Krishna : So by love he draws all men to Me—

Arjuna : And by compassion dissolves the moans of Maya—

Lord Krishna : Guiding mortal men to My immortal Self.

Arjuna : What if your Yogi fail my Lord?

Lord Krishna : No one who sets his foot once in the climb of My Yogas ever fails.

Arjuna : What if the imperfect Yogi attracted by Maya's call, in passion's heat, lusts unholy grip, and greed's grim craving, drop his holy staff?

Lord Krishna : No failure comes to any son of Yoga. For such an one is born again in virtue's home. Again he takes his staff and again he treads My paths!

Arjuna : If he again should fail?

Lord Krishna : Then from Life to Life I pursue him with My Yogas till he leaves the vacant halls of Maya. Neither life nor death interrupt the Yogi. Remember Arjuna there is no pause in My Yogas. From age to age I move with a thousand hands of My Love.

(*Exeunt Lord Krishna and Arjuna*).

SCENE VII

THE YOGA OF REALISATION

(*On the sixth day of the battle Arjuna is in morning meditation in a garden watching the sunrise*).

Arjuna : See the sunrise, my Lord, morning with dews, vapours, and the song of birds—the glad concomitants of a common dawn !

Lord Krishna : Common things are sublime Arjuna !

Arjuna : But sublime things are not common, my Lord.

Lord Krishna : In My Universe there is nothing high, nothing low, nothing common.

Arjuna : For your Universe is a secret Harmony—

Lord Krishna : Its secret am I.

Arjuna : Well then should I proceed to my questions ?

Lord Krishna : Yes.

Arjuna : I have heard from your dulcet lips of the Yogas of Work, Knowledge, Devotion, Meditation. Are these the part of the paths or the whole ?

Lord Krishna (Subtly) : Parts of the path which lead to the whole.

Arjuna : What is the Whole ?

Lord Krishna : I the Paramatma.

Arjuna : Declare to me Lord the nature of your mystic Self that lies beyond the reach of Works, Knowledge, Devotion, and Meditation.

Lord Krishna (Warning) : Concept cannot embrace Me. I am beyond Knowledge. Work cannot find Me. I am beyond Work. Devotion cannot clasp Me. I am beyond clasp. Meditation cannot pursue Me, I am beyond pursuit.

Arjuna (Despondent) : Then how shall I find you Lord ?

Lord Krishna : Step by step by the spiral stairways of Realisation.

Arjuna : What is Realisation ?

Lord Krishna : The Vision of the Truth through the grace of the Absolute.

Arjuna : Show me the truth of the Absolute.

Lord Krishna : Know first My double nature, veiled and unveiled.

Arjuna : What is your veiled nature ?

Lord Krishna : Illusion's field where body, mind and the Not-Self play in the masks and rounds of Maya—

Arjuna : Play of the mutable forms of the Absolute's life ?

Lord Krishna : The play of My Veils and not the play of the Real.

Arjuna : What is your unveiled nature ?

Lord Krishna : The nature of the changeless Atma which sees but is not bound by sight; which hears but is not bound by hearing; which moves but is not bound by motion; which is but is not bound by Being.

Arjuna : What is the work of your unveiled nature ?

Lord Krishna : The work of the Real.

Arjuna : What is the work of the Real.

Lord Krishna : The manifestations of My Veils.

Arjuna : What are the manifestations of your Veils ?

Lord Krishna : Body, mind, and the field of the Not-Self.

Arjuna : You are then the womb of Samsara's field—

Lord Krishna : And of all the fields that beyond Samsara lie.

Arjuna : You create and destroy and destroy and again create ?

Lord Krishna : From age to age, I build and unbuild My Universes. I am the First and the Last. I am the origin and the end.

Arjuna : What is your lowest manifestation ?

Lord Krishna : Matter.

Arjuna : Of what is matter composed ?

Lord Krishna : Of eight qualities, earth, water, fire, air, ether, life, mind, and the soul individual.

Arjuna : What is your essential nature ?

Lord Krishna : I am the All. Upon My thread drop bead by holy bead, My worlds, My Life, My creatures ! All is Mine. I am Ganga's holy wave. In sun and moon I am the Light. Of the Vedas I am the sacred syllable Aum. In the ether I am sound. In manhood I am man. In earth I am scent; in fire I am the flame; in power I am the power; in wisdom I am the wise. Know Me of all My kingdoms visible or invisible Master and Lord—

Arjuna : What of the three strands of Samsara which bind the lower self of man ?

Lord Krishna : Men they bind. Me they do not bind.

Arjuna : How do they bind ?

Lord Krishna : First the Sattwic man—virtue's child—beholds but a part of My veils. He sees and does not see. For his is Samsara' sight dazed in the twilight land of Maya. Next the Rajas man—passion's child—comes blinded by the mists of the illusions. He is a wanderer lost in the wilderness of the desires. For he is craving's son. Last with slow and halting steps arrives the soul of Tamas, darkness, moving in a whirl of dances from life to life in the cyclic rounds of the Illusions. The three strands of Samsara from Me come and to Me go. But they cannot hold Me. For I am the Transcendental.

Arjuna : What do the three strands do ?

Lord Krishna : Me they veil. My secret essence they hide.

Arjuna : Who may pierce the coverings of Samsara ?

Lord Krishna : All My votaries guided and guarded by My Light. For I alone am the remover of the veils.

Arjuna : What my Lord of those who are by your veils deluded ?

Lord Krishna : In the dens of darkness they must dwell till they learn to surrender to My Light.

Arjuna : What of those that seek in darkness your Light ?

Lord Krishna : Of such four classes clasp My Ray—first the man of holy worship; second the man who riches seeks; third the man of sorrow; and fourth the man of knowledge.

Arjuna : And which of these is in your heart of the first embrace ?

Lord Krishna : The man of knowledge in devotion merged in Me. His governed soul knows My way. From birth to birth he grows and in the end he comes to Me knowing in mortal garb the immortal Lord. With perfecting faith, Arjuna, he passes beyond the veils to Me. His aspirations I guide. In Me he finds the Lord of release.

Arjuna : How does your delusive power work in the heart of the deluded ?

Lord Krishna : Deluded men see Me not in the fogs of Maya. Listlessly they roam in search of Me. In Illusion's vale they find Me not. I am truth. How should they find truth in Illusion's dales ?

Arjuna : What hope for men deluded ?

Lord Krishna : By repeated births and deaths the deluded men abandon the road of the Illusions. In the cyclic progress of Time they come to grasp My changeless nature and veilless truth.

Arjuna : And what of your other votaries ?

Lord Krishna : All receive their merit due. No act of righteousness goes waste. My Justice stands firm, impartial as the sun that looks with equal eye upon the evil and the good and in My visitings of the human home certain as the revolution of the stars which wheel nightly around earth's cerulean blue.

Arjuna : What of those who circumambulate your altars muttering by rote their mystic hymns ?

Lord Krishna : Their rites of Nescience I accept.

Arjuna : What of those who adore the plural shapes of the Vedic divinities ?

Lord Krishna : Their worship I receive. Their Nescience I destroy.

Arjuna : What of those who worship the lesser gods ?

Lord Krishna : To the lesser gods they go.

Arjuna : What of those who worship the One ?

Lord Krishna : To the One they go.

Arjuna : Who spins the webs of Maya ?

Lord Krishna : I.

Arjuna : Who dissolves the webs of Maya ?

Lord Krishna : I.

Arjuna : For you are the Custodian of things?

Lord Krishna : Yes. For I am the All.

(*The dialogue closes in a hush as Arjuna realises the essential nature of the Paramatma*).

SCENE VIII

THE MYSTERY OF BRAHMA

(On the seventh day of the battle Arjuna at dawn is leaning over the edge of a rivulet dreaming of Brahma when Lord Krishna surprises him).

Lord Krishna : Arjuna !

Arjuna (Hearing) : My Lord did call me. I am here on the water's edge—

Lord Krishna : Dreaming by the river's lip—

Arjuna : Of Brahma, the Illimitable—

Lord Krishna : Seeking Him in the shadows of the waves ?

Arjuna : No my Lord, seeking Him in the wisdom of your lips—

Lord Krishna : Then ask your questions high.

Arjuna : What is Brahma ?

Lord Krishna : The Unconditioned Absolute.

Arjuna : Imperishable or perishable or both or beyond both ?

Lord Krishna : In his higher nature imperishable.

Arjuna : In his lower nature perishable ?

Lord Krishna : Yes.

Arjuna : In his transcendental nature beyond the imperishable and the perishable ?

Lord Krishna : Yes.

Arjuna : The Absolute cannot be perishable ?

Lord Krishna : No.

Arjuna : Then the Absolute seems to perish but does not perish ?

Lord Krishna : Yes.

Arjuna : Then his perishable nature is illusory ?

Lord Krishna : Yes.

Arjuna : Who creates the illusion ?

Lord Krishna : The dreaming mind of the Jiva.

Arjuna : When the Jiva wakes from the dream-state of Maya and when Nescience fades and knowledge arrives, does not the Jiva know that the perishable nature of the Absolute is the false ideation of the illusory Not-Self ?

Lord Krishna : Yes.

Arjuna : Then the Jiva beholds with true eyes the Imperishable Nature of the Absolute ?

Lord Krishna : Yes.

Arjuna : Is the Absolute bound by its nature higher or lower ?

Lord Krishna : No.

Arjuna : Brahma lies beyond the perishable and the imperishable ?

Lord Krishna : Yes.

Arjuna : Nature higher or lower has no appertainance to the Unknown ?

Lord Krishna : No.

Arjuna : Who has created the fiction of the perishable and the imperishable ?

Lord Krishna : The dreaming mind of the Jiva—

Arjuna : Thinking in fissions where no divisions are ?

Lord Krishna : Yes.

Arjuna : What then my Lord is Brahma ?

Lord Krishna : Brahma is the All.

Arjuna : The All is everywhere ?

Lord Krishna : Yes.

Arjuna : The All is therefore in Work, Knowledge, Devotion, and Sacrifice ?

Lord Krishna : Yes.

Arjuna : What enfolds the All ?

Lord Krishna : Nothing.

Arjuna : What does the All enfold ?

Lord Krishna : Everything.

Arjuna : What is the essential Self ?

Lord Krishna : The All.

Arjuna : What is the Not-Self ?

Lord Krishna : The illusory perception of the All-Self.

Arjuna : What is the Not-Self the effect of ?

Lord Krishna : The Power of the Maya of the All-Self.

Arjuna : Brahma is the Not-Self and the All-Self ?

Lord Krishna : For it is the All.

Arjuna : How do your Rishis reach the arcanum of the All-Self ?

Lord Krishna : By the repeated remembrance of the sacred Name of Brahma.

Arjuna : How do your Yogis leave the realms of birth ?

Lord Krishna : Repeating the sacred Syllable Aum, remembering

Me Brahma in the heart, exhaling the last sigh of the body My Yogis pass into My Light—

Arjuna : Where my Lord Krishna waits with healing in his hands for Samsara's wounds ?

Lord Krishna : Yes, such Rishis return no more to earth. For in Me they are emancipate. Ends for them Samsara's darkened road.

Arjuna : What of the Rishis who are not ripe for liberation ?

Lord Krishna : They are reborn for release.

Arjuna : When they have won their release ?

Lord Krishna : Then they go not back to earth.

Arjuna : When does the cycle of births cease ?

Lord Krishna : When the Yogi reaches the fields of the Unmanifest.

Arjuna : When does the field of your manifestation begin ?

Lord Krishna : When I manifest with worlds visible and invisible in a Day of Brahma.

Arjuna : How does your manifestation end ?

Lord Krishna : When I withdraw My manifestation in a Night of Brahma.

Arjuna : Are your manifestations of the Nights and Days of Brahma periodic ?

Lord Krishna : They are periodic. For I am Eternal Duration and Eternal Motion.

Arjuna : What is the duration of your manifestation called by your Yogis ?

Lord Krishna : Manvantara or Kalpa or Ages.

Arjuna : When the Kalpa opens then is a Day of Brahma ?

Lord Krishna : Yes.

Arjuna : When the Kalpa closes is a Night of Brahma ?

Lord Krishna : Yes.

Arjuna : The beginning and ending of your manifestations your Rishis name the Days and Nights of Brahma ?

Lord Krishna : Yes.

Arjuna : How long is a Day of Brahma ?

Lord Krishna : Incalculable ages.

Arjuna : But in mortalcal culation ?

Lord Krishna : A thousand years.

Arjuna : How long in mortal calculation is a Night of Brahma ?

Lord Krishna : A thousand years.

Arjuna : How does a Day of Brahma begin ?

Lord Krishna : By the sound of the Word of God.

Arjuna : What manifest ?

Lord Krishna : All the fields of the creation of the Kalpa—

Arjuna : Where in all Jivas evolve in the Period of a Day of Brahma ?

Lord Krishna : Yes.

Arjuna : For a Day of Brahma is the field of birth and re-birth ?

Lord Krishna : Yes.

Arjuna : When a Day of Brahma closes, then the fields of birth and re-birth close ?

Lord Krishna : For the Kalpa ends.

Arjuna : When does the Night of Brahma commence ?

Lord Krishna : When the Manvantara ends—

Arjuna : What happens in a Night of Brahma ?

Lord Krishna : All Life is re-absorbed into the Absolute—

Arjuna : And the Jivas of the prior Kalpa return to Brahma for rest ?

Lord Krishna : Yes.

Arjuna : For the first field of the first Kalpa is no more ?

Lord Krishna : Yes.

Arjuna : When does the Night of Brahma end ?

Lord Krishna : When another Day of Brahma begins—

Arjuna : Wherein the Jivas of the first Kalpa are re-born for evolution in the New Day of Brahma ?

Lord Krishna : Yes.

Arjuna : In the New Day a new field of manifestation opens ?

Lord Krishna : Yes. For the fields of births and re-births are renewed in matter and body new.

Arjuna : Then from Day to Night and from Night to Day, from renewal to rest and from rest to renewal, Kalpa after Kalpa, in eternal duration, the Jivas evolve on the road to God ?

Lord Krishna : Yes.

Arjuna : Wherein is the end of the road to God ?

Lord Krishna : In the eternal cycles in which there is no end—

Arjuna : For how can there be an end of Brahma's Life ?

Lord Krishna : Where does Brahma dwell, Arjuna ?

Arjuna : In the Lone beyond the manifest and the unmanifest.

Lord Krishna : For Brahma is the Lord of the Days and Nights of Brahma.

Arjuna : Tell me of the eternal road of birth and birthlessness which your Yogis tread.

Lord Krishna : By the bright road—the way of fire and flame—My Rishis go on the path of no-return. Them the cycles of re-birth no more bind. By the dark road—the way of the lunar light and the lunar gloom—My imperfect Yogis go from birth to birth aspiring for birthlessness. Both the paths are Mine. Both the paths lead to Me. More questions Arjuna ?

Arjuna : No. My Lord the discourse is done. Do I have your leave to retire ?

Lord Krishna : Yes. Farewell Arjuna.

Arjuna : Farewell my Lord till we meet again on the morrow.

(*Arjuna withdraws into a quiet to absorb the teachings of Lord Krishna*).

SCENE IX

RAJ YOGA

(On the eighth day of the battle at dusk Arjuna is meditating under the umbrage of a pine tree when Lord Krishna breaks upon his thoughts).

Lord Krishna : Prince of the magnanimous arms, for what do your noble lids search the nescient dust ?

Arjuna (Raising eyes of inquiry to Lord Krishna) : For the Science of Kings.

Lord Krishna : What is the Science of Kings ?

Arjuna : Raj Yoga. What is Raj Yoga, Lord ?

Lord Krishna : Raj Yoga is the comprehensive cognition of My Being, gross and subtle, visible and invisible, veiled or unveiled, in and beyond manifestation.

Arjuna : What is your gross being ?

Lord Krishna : The material manifestation of My bodies and minds incorporated in the lives of all My Jivas.

Arjuna : Your gross being is Maya ?

Lord Krishna : Maya to the thoughts of My Jivas but truths for the Absolute.

Arjuna : The worlds of illusion are not Illusion ?

Lord Krishna : In Me all the worlds of Illusion are Real. In My Jivas all the worlds of Illusion are Unreal. O Arjuna of the Intelligent glance, how should I the Real create the Unreal ?

Arjuna : Who creates the Unreal ?

Lord Krishna : The purblind mind of My Jivas !

Arjuna : For your Jivas are living creatures and therefore are free to create their worlds of Illusion—

Lord Krishna : In the limited ranges of My Maya, Arjuna—

Arjuna : And in the wider compass of your being they cannot create—

Lord Krishna : Or else their illusion would Me bind.

Arjuna : What then is Maya ?

Lord Krishna : The Face of Truth reversed—

Arjuna : Who reverses the fair Face of Truth ?

Lord Krishna : My Jivas.

Arjuna : Why ?

Lord Krishna : Because they wander from life to life on the rounds of Nescience ?

Arjuna : What is Nescience ?

Lord Krishna : The dreams of My Jivas in the dusk of Nescience.

Arjuna : How do you rouse your Jivas from the dreams of the dusk ?

Lord Krishna : By the stresses of My mystic Light—

Arjuna : Whose repetitive taps restore the Jivas to your Truth ?

Lord Krishna : Leading them back reluctant or acquiescent from the Unreal to the Real.

Arjuna : For you are the feet that follow—

Lord Krishna : And the hound that sues—

Arjuna : And the Power that grips the Jivas with the grip of the Absolute—

Lord Krishna : So that none perishes.

Arjuna : What is your subtle being ?

Lord Krishna : I am the Changeless Paramatma—

Arjuna : Watching mutation but from mutation free—

Lord Krishna : Making Maya and therefore of Maya liberate.

Arjuna : For how should the Master of Maya be subservient to Maya ?

Lord Krishna : For I make and break Maya. I am Truth.

Arjuna : What is your visible being ?

Lord Krishna : The body, mind, and matter of My Jivas.

Arjuna : What is your invisible being ?

Lord Krishna : I am the imperishable Atma concealed in the material embodiments of My Jivas.

Arjuna : What in the Jivas perish ?

Lord Krishna : Their material embodiments.

Arjuna : Why ?

Lord Krishna : To reveal the secrecies of the Atma.

Arjuna : What in the Jivas does not perish ?

Lord Krishna : The immortal Atma.

Arjuna : What is your veiled being ?

Lord Krishna : The body, mind and matter of My Jivas.

Arjuna : Wherefore are your veils ?

Lord Krishna : My veils are for the evolution of My Jivas from Life to Life till the bonds of birth and death are ended.

Arjuna : What if your veils were withdrawn ?

Lord Krishna : Then My Jivas could not evolve.

Arjuna : Who makes the veils ?

Lord Krishna : The collective concourse of My monads.

Arjuna : What is your veilless being ?

Lord Krishna : The being of the Absolute which is not being.

Arjuna : What is the Absolute ?

Lord Krishna : The Unknown—

Arjuna : How is the Absolute grasped by man ?

Lord Krishna : By its Manifestations.

Arjuna : What are the Manifestations of the Absolute ?

Lord Krishna : My Manvantaras, Kalpas, or Ages—

Arjuna : Which open and close the shows of the Absolute ?

Lord Krishna : Yes.

Arjuna : What is your complete being ?

Lord Krishna : Paramatma—

Arjuna : Which is Eternal Duration, Eternal Motion, and Eternal Manifestation from Manvantara to Manvantara ?

Lord Krishna : Yes.

Arjuna : Where are the halls of the Paramatma ?

Lord Krishna : Beyond manifestation's ken.

Arjuna : What do men see in you my Lord Krishna ?

Lord Krishna : Some see in Me the mortal body alone—

Arjuna : Such men are by delusion bound—

Lord Krishna : For they rove blind in Maya's round—

Arjuna : Missing the Atma which their bodies enfold—

Lord Krishna : Losing in the mortal form the immortal soul—

Arjuna : Such men are beasts and demons caught in the webs of Maya—

Lord Krishna : Whose works are vain—

Arjuna : Whose toils end in Maya's pain—

Lord Krishna : For such men are doomed to death in Illusion's ground of burning. But other men know Me as the Atma—

Arjuna : The moveless motion in the lives of your Jivas—

Lord Krishna : The secret evolver of the secret Cycles—

Arjuna : Lord of Life—

Lord Krishna : Master of works—

Arjuna : King of the Sacrifice—

Lord Krishna : Sovereign of Knowledge—

Arjuna : The affluent receiver of all worship.

Lord Krishna : I am the temple and the taper in the temple. I am the altar, the smoke, and the fire of all My shrines. I am the cinder of the funeral Pyre ; fat of the flame ; incense of the Sacrifice ; robe of the acolyte ; staff of the Sannyasin ; prayer of the holy lip. I am the hymn of the morning and the song of Vesper. I am Aum. I am Rig-Veda ; Sama-Veda ; Yajur-Veda ; knowledge of the Way ; parent of the Word ; Sire of the Rishis ; Witness of the work ; Judge of the deed ; and the Shelter of all souls. I am the Seven Angels of the ascent ; the Seven Lucifers of the fall ; the Seven darknesses of hell and the Seven lights of heaven. I am the Seven Seas ; the Seven Earths ; the Seven Skies ; the Seven Shadows and the Seven Substances. I am the Seven Gems and the Seven Treasuries of the Invisible. I am the First and the Last ; the Beginning and the End. I am the All.

Arjuna : What do your mystics call you ?

Lord Krishna : The Great Breath.

Arjuna : For you are Life—

Lord Krishna : For I am Death which is the fullest Life.

Arjuna : What of your worshippers ?

Lord Krishna : My worshippers go the way their worship goes.

Arjuna : Determined by merit—

Lord Krishna : Determined by the Karmic Law which is above merit.

Arjuna : Where do the worshippers of images go ?

Lord Krishna : To the world of images.

Arjuna : What are the world of images ?

Lord Krishna : The inner worlds of Maya.

Arjuna : Where do the worshippers of the lower deities go ?

Lord Krishna : To the lower deities.

Arjuna : Where do the worshippers of the higher divinities go ?

Lord Krishna : To the higher divinities.

Arjuna : Where do the worshippers of the One go ?

Lord Krishna : To Krishna.

Arjuna : What is devotion ?
Lord Krishna : My path of Love.
Arjuna : What is the fruit of devotion ?
Lord Krishna : My release—
Arjuna : Which is Peace.
Lord Krishna : Yes.
Arjuna : Who are your devotees ?
Lord Krishna : All.
Arjuna : The high and the low ?
Lord Krishna : My favour knows neither high nor low.
Arjuna : Of the four castes which do you repel ?
Lord Krishna : None. All are Mine.
Arjuna : And what of the Sudra caste ?
Lord Krishna : Their humility I receive and their pride I break with low work for the Spirit's Progress from life to life.
Arjuna : What of the woman lost ?
Lord Krishna : Her virtue I reestablish in wombs of new birth.
Arjuna : What gifts do you reject ?
Lord Krishna : None. All gifts are Mine.
Arjuna : A leaf, a fruit, a flower, a tear—
Lord Krishna : All offerings are Mine.
Arjuna : Wide is the heart of my Lord Krishna—
Lord Krishna : Wider than all My heavens—
Arjuna : And larger than all your skies—
Lord Krishna : For I am Infinity.
Arjuna : Into your Infinite embrace I come—
Lord Krishna : Arjuna come.
Arjuna : Will my Lord keep his tryst ?
Lord Krishna : What tryst ?
Arjuna (Ardently seeking) : Show me the Face of the Absolute.
Lord Krishna : The climax of the climaxes of My Yoga ?
Arjuna : Yes.
Lord Krishna : I will Arjuna—
Arjuna : At the occult hour ?
Lord Krishna : Yes.
Arjuna : My Lord I wait.

(*Arjuna remains in silence and Lord Krishna withdraws for the assimilation of his teachings*).

SCENE X

THE SUPERNAL MANIFESTATIONS

(*On the ninth day of the battle, Arjuna is resting by a water-fall when Lord Krishna surprises him*).

Lord Krishna : A water-fall ! Resting Arjuna ?

Arjuna (Surprised) : My Lord—

Lord Krishna : Why, did I break upon your repose ?

Arjuna : No, my noble Lord.

Lord Krishna : What at noonday hold your lids in quiet ?

Arjuna : The Mysteries of the Manifestations of Brahma.

Lord Krishna : Part or whole of My many shapes and forms ?

Arjuna : The Whole.

Lord Krishna : O Purblind eye of Maya, how would you grasp My whole ?

Arjuna : Then enumerate the parts—

Lord Krishna : Which will reveal the mastered principles of the whole ?

Arjuna : Yes.

Lord Krishna : I was before Time was—

Arjuna : Therefore the sons of Time may know you not ?

Lord Krishna : Yes. I was before Space was—

Arjuna : Therefore the sons of Space may comprehend you not ?

Lord Krishna : Yes. I was before My manifestation was—

Arjuna : Therefore no son of manifestation can seize the roll of your ancient being?

Lord Krishna : Yes. Yet know My truth from Me the Truth. I am beyond birth and death, beyond all beginnings and all endings, Lord of the seven heavens, and Master of all My Rishis. I am wisdom and austerity, release and peace, the seed and germ of all My Manifestations. Of Me were born the seven seers, the four Ancients and the holy Manus. They knew the plurality of My Being. Me the Transcendental and Immanent they beheld in subtle states of trance. Me they saw as the origin and dissolution of all things from Kalpa to Kalpa. Me they knew as the Lamp of Knowledge. Me they marked as the Flame no larger than a finger's breadth in the heart's central shrine—

Arjuna : For all your renowned Rishis had by Yoga's discipline rare reached the last Arcadia of your Lights.

Lord Krishna : Narada, Asita, Devala, Vyasa, Yogis old, had seen Me in lucid trance—

Arjuna : How had they known you ?

Lord Krishna : As the Ancient of Days, the Primaeval Being, neither begetting nor begotten, the One without a second, the Lone in multitudinous shapes beyond count or number manifest. Which then of My Aspects should I to you unfold ?

Arjuna : Portions of your many veils.

Lord Krishna : Partial views of the impartible Whole ?

Arjuna : Yes. In brief review the ranges of your forms manifold.

Lord Krishna : I am the Cosmic Substance of all My Kalpas without bound or limit. I am the Paramatma—the One Community of subtle essence which lies in the hearts of all unperceived. I am the Beginning, the Middle and the End of all things. Of the sunlight I am the Sun. Of the moonlight, I am the Moon. Of the starlight, I am the Star. Of the twilight, I am the Morn. Of the dawn, I am the Day. Of Nights and Days, I am the Eternities. Of the Vedas, I am the Sama-Veda. Of Samsara, I am the Truth. Of destruction, I am the Lord. Of creation, I am the Master. Of preservation, I am the guard. Of priests, I am the Lama. Of temples, I am the Light. Of the seas, I am the Ocean. Of mountains, I am the peak of Meru. Of the armouries of heaven, I am the thunderbolt and light. I am the Whole.

Arjuna (Now in the unitary consciousness): Of your many forms I see but One—

Lord Krishna : When you see the One do you not see the Whole ?

Arjuna : Yes.

Lord Krishna (Stimulating the unitary consciousness by his subtle rays) : When you see the Whole, do you not see the parts ?

Arjuna : Yes. For the whole is the part and the part is the whole. What is division and what is synthesis ?

Lord Krishna : Division is the sight of Samsara and Synthesis is the sight of the Spirit. Both division and synthesis am I.

Arjuna : Are you Affirmation or Negation or both or beyond ?

Lord Krishna : I am the Grand Negation. I am Neti, Neti, Neti. I am not within Nescience's bounds or the mind's embrace. I am the Grand Affirmation. I am. I am. I am. I am beyond Affirmation and Negation. For I am the All that All transcends.

Arjuna (Pondering) : What is Evil my Lord ?

Lord Krishna : My Good unevolved.

Arjuna : What is Good ?

Lord Krishna : Aspiration unfulfilled.

Arjuna : What is beyond the pair of the Opposites ?

Lord Krishna : I.

Arjuna : Who has created Evil ?

Lord Krishna : Man's deeds and Man's Karma.

Arjuna : Who has created Virtue ?

Lord Krishna : I.

Arjuna : For what end ?

Lord Krishna : For the release of My votaries.

Arjuna : Who is the Arch-betrayer ?

Lord Krishna (Smiling) : I.

Arjuna : Whom do you betray ?

Lord Krishna : Him who betrays Me.

Arjuna : In pursuance of the Karmic Law ?

Lord Krishna : Yes. He that betrays Me is himself betrayed.

Arjuna : Who is the Arch-deceiver ?

Lord Krishna (Again smiling) : I.

Arjuna : Whom do you deceive ?

Lord Krishna : The sinner steeped in sin.

Arjuna : How is the sinner arraigned ?

Lord Krishna : By the Law of Karma.

Arjuna (Suspecting) : Do you assume the demon's mask ?

Lord Krishna : Yes.

Arjuna : Wherefore ?

Lord Krishna (Again smiling) : In order all demons to destroy.

Arjuna : For what end ?

Lord Krishna : For Virtue's regeneration.

Arjuna : My Lord you have answered all my interrogations.

Lord Krishna : Should we retire ?

Arjuna : Yes my Lord. The noonday sun is warm.

(*Arjuna moves away in a solemn mood*).

SCENE XI

THE VISION OF THE ABSOLUTE FORM

(*On the tenth night of the battle, Arjuna at midnight is waiting for Lord Krishna in the Temple of Kali expectant of the Supernal Vision promised him. He hears footsteps and challenges the guard on duty*).

Arjuna : Who goes there ?

Guard : I the guard of the first watch—

Arjuna : Where is my Lord Krishna ?

Guard : Most prompt upon the hour will he come.

Arjuna : What time is it ?

Guard : Midnight.

Arjuna : Report when his footsteps pass the dews.

Guard : My Lord I will.

Arjuna : Bring me no communications to-night.

Guard : Business will await you on the morrow ?

Arjuna : Yes. I wish to be alone with my Lord Krishna this night.

Guard : Do I have your leave to withdraw ?

Arjuna : Yes. Did I hear a sound ?

Guard : It was the wind stirring in the trees—

Arjuna : Not the soft pacings of My Lord Krishna ?

Guard : No.

Arjuna (Speaking to himself as the guard has withdrawn) : Bright is the moonlight on this sward. The moon is full. Some say that the full moon is the esoteric hour when God whispers to the souls He loves. What hush is this ? What spell about my mind plays ? Me thinks soon some magic presence will be nigh—

Lord Krishna (Coming unmarked from behind) : Arjuna !

Arjuna : My Lord is here—

Lord Krishna : Do I upon your peace intrude ?

Arjuna : No, this is the promised interlude of the sight and show of My Lord Krishna's form in the shrine of Kali—

Lord Krishna (Testing) : Did you think that My appointment I had missed ?

Arjuna : No, my Lord, how could you forget your promised tryst ?

Lord Krishna : Should I now to your eyes give reprieve of Maya's misty sight ?

Arjuna : Yes. For to see is to believe.

Lord Krishna : For merely to hear My doctrines is not to know the counterfeits of My Illusion's Show.

Arjuna : Then for hearing substitute the Vision of the Absolute !

Lord Krishna : But dear Spirit Arjuna, already I see your hair rise in holy terror and your lowered lids with horror tremble.

Arjuna (Confessing) : How should I my fears dissemble ?

Lord Krishna (In secret operation with his rays) : Well, then by My mystic spells I your eyes unseal—

Arjuna (Affected by the occult rays) : O holy Light, the forms of the Absolute reveal !

Lord Krishna : By the touch of My esoteric Ray, see what no mortal lid yet has seen—shapes of the Universal Lord hiding behind the screen of the flesh held in the grip of Maya's subtle net, the rare splendour of My Light—

Arjuna : Too bright for mine eyes, too bright !

Lord Krishna (Watching Arjuna's nervous reactions) : Do you still wish to remain in Maya's night ?

Arjuna : No. Yet touch not my lids with your esoteric Light.

Lord Krishna (Warning) : Beware of My Ray more luminous than the shine of the sun. Ah, why shake your limbs before My work is begun ?

Arjuna (Terrified) : In terror I withdraw—

Lord Krishna (Holding Arjuna with his eyes) : In error you recede—

Arjuna (Retreating in fear) : With prayer I intercede ! Abrogate not my fleshly sight.

Lord Krishna (Struggling with Arjuna) : But the tryst ?

Arjuna (Pleading) : Bring me back to Maya's mist.

Lord Krishna : Fear not, the sting of God is the kiss of the Nirvanic Bliss. There ! (Striking with the light) With My radiant air your sight I tear ! Behold the Absolute !

Arjuna (Shrieking) : My Lord I am blinded !

Lord Krishna : Arjuna, you see !

Arjuna (Healed) : I yield. O God, I behold the Absolute's holy field !

Lord Krishna : Say what you see !

Arjuna : With wide amaze I gaze upon the body of God !

Lord Krishna : In the body of God what do you behold ?

Arjuna : Many eyes, many hands, many mouths, many limbs, many worlds, many Spirits, lords of heaven and lords of hell, which crówd upon crowd usurp the shoreless shores of the Absolute !

Lord Krishna : What is in the Northern sky !

Arjuna : God !

Lord Krishna : What is in the South ?

Arjuna : God !

Lord Krishna : What is in the West ?

Arjuna : God !

Lord Krishna : What is in the East ?

Arjuna : God !

Lord Krishna : Who is the Lord of the North, the South, the West and the East ?

Arjuna : God !

Lord Krishna : Who is the regent of the four quarters of the sky ?

Arjuna : God !

Lord Krishna : Who is the Lord of the Seven Directions ?

Arjuna : God !

Lord Krishna : Who is beyond the Seven Directions ?

Arjuna : God !

Lord Krishna : What do you behold in the field of Time ?

Arjuna : The roll of the illimitable worlds of Time.

Lord Krishna : And beyond ?

Arjuna : Illimitable worlds beyond the Rings of Time.

Lord Krishna : What do you behold in the field of Space ?

Arjuna : Creatures of all the worlds of Space.

Lord Krishna : And beyond ?

Arjuna : Worlds of the Spaceless and creatures of the Spaceless—

Lord Krishna : Moving in the rounds of the Eternities ?

Arjuna : Yes.

Lord Krishna : What else do you see ?

Arjuna : The One.

Lord Krishna : Who is the One?

Arjuna : The Lord of the worlds.

Lord Krishna : What does he bear in his hands ?

Arjuna : The mace of Power.

Lord Krishna : And on his brow what lies ?

Arjuna : The coronet of creation.

Lord Krishna : What beside him flashes ?

Arjuna : Brahma's Throne of Power which engirdles the heavens and the earth.

Lord Krishna : Where is the Throne of Brahma ?

Arjuna : In the viewless air.

Lord Krishna : Then with undimmed eyes declare what you perceive beside the sovereign seat of Brahma ?

Arjuna : Fire !

Lord Krishna : Fire in the earth, fire in the heavens and fire beyond the earths and the heavens.

Arjuna : For the Lord of the Worlds, is He not Fire ?

Lord Krishna : Yes, Fire brighter than the shine of a thousand suns. What is in My Fire Arjuna ?

Arjuna : The All.

Lord Krishna : What lie in the halls of My Fire ?

Arjuna : Your Adepts, Seers, Initiates, Angels, Demons, Spirits, men and souls I perceive as the forms of your Fire.

Lord Krishna : What do you perceive beyond the forms of Fire ?

Arjuna : Other worlds.

Lord Krishna : What other worlds ?

Arjuna : Other worlds of Formless Fire.

Lord Krishna : In the apocalypse of the senses, Arjuna, Fairy Spirit to My bosom dear, know that you are flame and fire inurned for a while in form but here and now from formal sight by Me released—

Arjuna : My Lord sightless I see—

Lord Krishna : Krishna and the forms of Krishna with orbless eyes behold— a rare vision to my dear Prince given.

Arjuna : Sign of the Lord of the Worlds and the love of heaven !

(*Suddenly the clouds of Maya enfold the Temple of Kali which disappears. The mists of illusion re-form from which emerges the Temple of Discord where King Dhritarashtra and his counsellor Samjaya are meditating in silence*).

Dhritarashtra : Why this silence Samjaya ?

Samjaya : The fumes choke my eyes.

Dhritarashtra : Why this long pause ?

Samjaya : Let patience my Lord be your stay. For I begin to see. Forms my Lord (Excited). There, there ! Illusion, hold !

Dhritarashtra : What form ?

Samjaya : The royal Temple of Kali surcharged with Light.

Dhritarashtra : Who move within its imperial precincts at midnight ?

Samjaya : My Lord Krishna and by him in yellow vesture clad in Sannyasin's robe—our Prince Arjuna.

Dhritarashtra : What Spirits do they invoke in the black watch of night ?

Samjaya : No, Spirits my Lord. Bright forms I see—brighter than the solar rays.

Dhritarashtra : What is Prince Arjuna doing ?

Samjaya : The Prince is stilled in Cosmic Trance.

Dhritarashtra : How proceeds the Cosmic dream ?

Samjaya (Perceiving the truth) : My Lord there is no Cosmic dream. The Real moves with the silent steps of the Real.

Dhritarashtra : Speak and report.

Samjaya : I see a body which many bodies enclose. I see light within light and form within form.

Dhritarashtra : What are the lights and what the forms ?

Samjaya : The lights are the lights of My Lord Krishna and the forms are the forms of the Lord of the Light.

Dhritarashtra : You behold a blaze—

Samjaya : Yes, a blaze of a million beams which blasts the sight.

Dhritarashtra : What do you see in the blaze ?

Samjaya : My Lord Krishna—

Dhritarashtra : Perfumed with unguents ?

Samjaya : Yes.

Dhritarashtra : Enfolded in flowers ?

Samjaya : Yes.

Dhritarashtra : Gemmed ?

Samjaya : Gemmed from head to foot.

Dhritarashtra : What does he wear ?

Samjaya : Vestures of light.

Dhritarashtra : Within his incorporeal mould what do you see ?

Samjaya : The Cosmic Vision.

Dhritarashtra : What do you behold in the Cosmic Vision ?

Samjaya : Many lips, many eyes, many hands, many orbs, many gods, many demons, many beings, a plenitude of forms—

Dhritarashtra (In awe) : Forms of the Absolute Whole without division or part !

Samjaya : Yes.

Dhritarashtra : Can you see the countenance of my Lord Krishna ?

Samjaya : Yes.

Dhritarashtra : In peace ?

Samjaya : In peace profound.

Dhritarashtra : Is my Lord Krishna armed ?

Samjaya : Armed to the teeth.

Dhritarashtra (Apprehending) : Any threat to the Kurus ?

Samjaya : I cannot say. But look, my Lord, look. The Forms steal from the temple. Ghostly illusions stop !

Dhritarashtra : Do not bar their way. They are as the air intangible.

Samjaya : Majestical forms stay !

Dhritarashtra : Nay, let them depart from night's dews. The daylight they will not endure. Release the forms !

Samjaya : My Lord as air they go !

Dhritarashtra : Let them go.

Samjaya : My Lord the mists again !

Dhritarashtra : Disperse the mists. Put out the light in the Temple of Discord.

Samjaya : Why my Lord ?

Dhritarashtra : My mind is by tumult crossed—

Samjaya : Patience my Lord. Cool patience bathe your brows.

Dhritarashtra : My blind eyes too clearly see. The war of the Kurus clan is lost.

Samjaya : My Lord and King speak not so.

Dhritarashtra : In the shrine I say. Put out the glow.

Samjaya : From the temple my Lord let us go.

Dhritarashtra : Yes. What blows await us I do not know.

(*The mists of Maya cover the Temple of Discord which suddenly disappears. From rare rising clouds emerges the Temple of Kali where Prince Arjuna and Lord Krishna are still in session*).

Arjuna : Is this incense or is this mist which veils my eyes in vapour thick—

Lord Krishna : Do not trouble your mind with occult phenomena. Move to the reaches of My Light. (Striking) Once more open with novel sight !

Arjuna : My Lord !

Lord Krishna : What is the matter ?

Arjuna : That stab my Lord !

Lord Krishna : The wound of the Light ?

Arjuna : Yes.

Lord Krishna (Smilingly) : What wound ?

Arjuna (Taken by surprise) : My Lord again I see !

Lord Krishna : What do you see ?

Arjuna : The aureate body of my Lord Krishna !

Lord Krishna : And in the body of gold what do you behold ?

Arjuna : The Infinite's forms manifold.

Lord Krishna : Into one Form resolved and rolled ?

Arjuna : Yes.

Lord Krishna : Arms, eyes and lips of all My Beings untold which dwell in the swell of My unplumbed deeps—

Arjuna : Deeps without bounds—

Lord Krishna : Beyond the rounds of Mind or the silent sounds of Senses where the Real in peaceful murmurs sweeps the seas of Eternity—where worlds within worlds of the Absolute lapse upon the shoals of Infinity—

Arjuna : Whose Timeless lids embrace in wide and endless circuits god, demons and angels—

Lord Krishna : Lords of the Storm, Lords of the Doom, Lords of the Solar Ray—

Arjuna : And the Lords of the Dim who hide in the veils of the Day—

Lord Krishna : Aye, the Lords of the Gloom in the womb of the earth whom all flesh fears in the nescient night of the dust—

Arjuna (Seeing the form of Kali) : Help Lord ! What dread shape with teeth and lips and eyes agape moves towards my lids ? Horrid form avaunt ! There is no room for thee here ! This is the shrine of Light !

Lord Krishna : Courage Arjuna. Do not strike that shape. It is invulnerable.

Arjuna (Perturbed) : What form is that ?

Lord Krishna (Disarming Arjuna) : It is my demon Death.

Arjuna (Trembling) : The vision of Kali the destroyer ?

Lord Krishna : Yes.

Arjuna : From her black eyes my eyes revert !

Lord Krishna : Kali will do you no hurt.

Arjuna : Remove the spell my Lord.

Lord Krishna (Explaining) : I am Kali. I am Time. I am change. I am the scythe that reaps, the corn that is reaped and the harvest that is garnered in the catacombs of My Eternities. Fear not Me, sweet Arjuna.

Arjuna (Shrinking from the sight) : Yet shield me from Kali's eyes which make the triple worlds tremble.

Lord Krishna : Kali is My Light.

Arjuna (Afraid) : My Lord, I see no glow in that shadow dark.

Lord Krishna : Do you not know that in My holy Spark all shadows vanish ?

Arjuna : That darkling shadow from my eyes banish ! Is not Kali death ?

Lord Krishna : Is not death life ?

Arjuna (In throes of fear) : Yet I will not see !

Lord Krishna : Then look at Me and not on Kali. My deep wisdom weigh. Know that Kali the destroyer is Krishna the Creator. For by destruction alone are my new kingdoms of creation born.

Arjuna (Beginning to understand) : As from night's dark womb comes the silver morn—

Lord Krishna : As from twilight and dusk comes the dawn !

Now brighten eyes ! Be at peace. Kali is My creature of Death.

Arjuna : Whom will you destroy ?

Lord Krishna (Severely) : The Kurus.

Arjuna (Seeing the coming destruction) : Do my lids betray ?

Lord Krishna : No, my truth you see today.

Arjuna : My Lord the Doom approaches.

Lord Krishna : My Time moves to slay.

Arjuna (Still uncertain) : Whom ?

Lord Krishna : The Kurus. Not one shall live. See the flood of My destruction's Ray. Where is Duryodhana ?

Arjuna (Looking into the Cosmic Mirror) : In the bunker of his chancellery dead !

Lord Krishna : Where are Drona, Bhisma, Karna, the mighty warriors of the Kurus ?

Arjuna (Shocked) : All dead !

Lord Krishna : Whom have you to slay ?

Arjuna : None.

Lord Krishna : For Kurukshetra's battle in My Cosmic halls is won.

Arjuna : Yet, Lord, Kali's dread cowl remove.

Lord Krishna (With finger on lip) : Hush ! The occult secret. Arjuna ! I am Kali's raven cowl and hood—

Arjuna (Understanding) : The deft destroyer of the evil—

Lord Krishna : And the just guardian of the good. Ere I dissolve the cosmic clarities of your eye, advance your lashes thither (Pointing to Kali's mouth).

Arjuna (Looking into Kali's mouth) : My Lord, Lord—

Lord Krishna : Well, what do you see ?

Arjuna : As a loud torrent from a mountain-head with fretful foam intolerant of boulders leaps from waterfall to waterfall into a darkened ravine, so the host of the Kurus frenzy-driven race into the mouth of Kali—

Lord Krishna : Whose munching teeth crunch their corpses—

Arjuna : And whose hungry lips draw all men to the jaws of death—

Lord Krishna : As a moth around a candle, the Kurus enring the flames of Kali. One by one singed and burnt they die. For Kali is My Asura of death—

Arjuna (Retreating from the mouth of hell) : Horrible ! Horrible ! Horrible ! Take away these eyes. My Lord, your former shape resume.

Lord Krishna (Striking) : Once more I ply My lightening's task !

Arjuna (Coming down from Cosmic trance) : Where am I ? Where is gone Kali's mask ? Is this daylight ?

Lord Krishna (With soothing touch) : Heed. Here am I Arjuna !

Arjuna (Awakening) : In your earthly body renewed, if my eyes deceive me not ?

Lord Krishna : Yes, restored and renewed—

Arjuna (Repentant) : My Lord, how rude have I been to you, how rude.

Lord Krishna : Now you will know Me as you have never known.

Arjuna : As the Cosmic Lord in the mortal garb concealed—

Lord Krishna : By My Cosmic Light were your lids unsealed—

Arjuna : And by your rich Ray were the forms of the Absolute revealed.

Lord Krishna : And by My Lightening's subtle stroke have I brought you back safe to the dark dells of the dust ?

Arjuna (In gratitude) : Salutation to the Lord of the dust. Hail Vayu (Wind), Yama (Death), Varuna(Sky), Agni (Fire), hail !

Lord Krishna : Neither the teaching of the Vedas, nor austerities, nor charity, nor sacrifice, avail to show the sights which to you have been shown.

Arjuna : By the Grace of the Paramatma, have I seen this strange spectacle of Hell and Heaven.

Lord Krishna : To no other man has such grace been given Arjuna.

Arjuna : Gratitude Lord for the latitude of your teachings.

Lord Krishna : My wisdom is large and My heart is wide.

Arjuna : In that wisdom and in that heart, O Lord, may I reside—

Lord Krishna (In a voice of awe) : Reside !

Arjuna : Bright my Lord shine upon me your lids Divine.

Lord Krishna : Then Arjuna fight.

Arjuna (Rising in courage) : I doff my yellow robe and put my armoured jerkin on—

Lord Krishna : For Me strive and fight !

Arjuna : No craven fear holds my heart. I the slayer go to slay with no murder on my hands—

Lord Krishna : For the Kurus have by Me been slain.

Arjuna : To you my Lord Krishna the laurels of war I resign—

Lord Krishna : Yours is the victory over the Kurus decreed by My Will Divine.

(*Arjuna and Lord Krishna slowly withdraw from the Temple*).

SCENE XII

BHAKTI YOGA

(On the eleventh day of the battle Arjuna is watching from a mound the movement "Operation Battle—Axe" directed to the capture of the Capital of the Kurus. Lord Krishna in accord with his promise is arranging the strategy of the Pandavas with silent psychic forces. Arjuna joyously addresses Lord Krishna).

Arjuna : Our troops are deploying on the terrain—

Lord Krishna : Let them move faster Arjuna on the Kurus' proud domain.

Arjuna : Speed my lord ?

Lord Krishna : Speed is the new strategy of war—

Arjuna : Turn the flanks ?

Lord Krishna : With your tanks cross the vacant trenches—

Arjuna : And from the rear surprise the eyes of the camp of the Kurus—

Lord Krishna : Seizing in his Headquarters Duryodhana alive or dead.

Arjuna : Such instructions I have already delivered to our High Command.

Lord Krishna : Then the Operation Battle—Axe proceeds upon these instructions—

Arjuna : Yes. I have reports in my hands which confirm that our forces move in accordance with those plans.

Lord Krishna : What do you through your glasses view?

Arjuna : The reeling ranks of the Kurus circled in the rear by our arriving infantry with the full support—

Lord Krishna : Of your planes and tanks ?

Arjuna : Yes, the combined attack by land and air—

Lord Krishna : What are those silken mushrooms and dangling threads ?

Arjuna : The air-drop behind the supply lines of the Kurus.

Lord Krishna : What of the roads ?

Arjuna : They are crammed with burning vehicles.

Lord Krishna : And their Headquarters ?

Arjuna : Encompassed by the turrets of a hundred tanks.

Lord Krishna : And their artillery ?

Arjuna : It is silenced.

Lord Krishna : And their strong points ?

Arjuna : Overrun, captured or destroyed.

Lord Krishna : Who mans their trenches ?

Arjuna (Smiling) : My Lord the Kurus are on the run—

Lord Krishna : And your prison camps ?

Arjuna : Full to the brim. Booty and prisoners we have without number.

Lord Krishna : Does the Law of God sleep or slumber ?

Arjuna : No, my Lord.

Lord Krishna (In a warning voice) : My Cosmic Law to judgement due proceeds—

Arjuna : The answer of the Karmic Lords of deeds for deeds.

Lord Krishna (Predicting) : The battle of the Kurus and the Pandavas ends on Kurukshetra's baleful field.

Arjuna : My Lord who may with you for Mercy plead ?

Lord Krishna : Judgement I hold in My holy hands. No mercy Arjuna for the Kurus. From harsh Kurukshetra's plains the Kurus recoil.

Arjuna (Realising) : My Lord, of the arts of war you are the consummate Master—

Lord Krishna : Aye the Sovereign of the Sacred Field and the Lord of all disaster—

Arjuna : Now my Lord may I from this mound descend ?

Lord Krishna (Catching the hint) : To sit beside Me in the shade—

Arjuna : Lofty themes discussing—

Lord Krishna : For the summer sun is high and the rain-clouds of July have not yet released their showers on the parched plains—

Arjuna (Indicating) : This way my Lord to the umbrage—

Lord Krishna : Here in this jasmin bower let us sit. More questions Arjuna ?

Arjuna : Yes.

Lord Krishna : What questions ?

Arjuna : Which is the easier way—the way of Love or the way of thought ?

Lord Krishna : Bhakti Yoga and Raj Yoga both lead to Me.

Arjuna : Which is the gentler ascent ?

Lord Krishna : Few may climb the steeps of Raj Yoga seeking in abstract contemplation Me the Brahma Immanent and transcendental in the subtle fields of My manifestations deep. Hard is the way of the philosophic vision; frore the air; perilous the steps for him who would Parabrahma know. What flesh may tread without tremor the heights of the All ? What foot but slips on the icy precipices of the Supreme ?

Arjuna : What of the slope of Devotion's road ?

Lord Krishna : Light is the slope of Love, rich its air and abundant its releases. For are not all the roads to God the road of Love ?

Arjuna : What is the first release of Love ?

Lord Krishna : Through Work for Me—

Arjuna : Works without fruit for you ?

Lord Krishna : Yes.

Arjuna : Work without desire for you ?

Lord Krishna : Yes.

Arjuna : Is such work work ?

Lord Krishna : No. Work which is work for love, is not work but Love.

Arjuna : Then through Love, work ceases ?

Lord Krishna : Yes.

Arjuna : When work ceases what remains ?

Lord Krishna : Love.

Arjuna : And what is Love ?

Lord Krishna : The first release.

Arjuna : What is the second release of Love ?

Lord Krishna : Through Knowledge seeking Me.

Arjuna : What is the fruit of Knowledge ?

Lord Krishna : I.

Arjuna : What are you ?

Lord Krishna : Love.

Arjuna : What is true Knowledge then ?

Lord Krishna : Love.

Arjuna : What is the second release through Knowledge ?

Lord Krishna : Love.

Arjuna : Then Work and Knowledge are both Love ?

Lord Krishna : Yes.

Arjuna : What is Meditation on my Lord ?

Lord Krishna : Love.

Arjuna : What is the release of Meditation ?

Lord Krishna : Love.

Arjuna : What are Worship and Sacrifice for my Lord ?

Lord Krishna : Love.

Arjuna : What is the release of adoration and Sacrifice for my Lord ?

Lord Krishna : Love.

Arjuna : Then Love is the summary of all the ways to God ?

Lord Krishna : Yes. For God is Love.

Arjuna : What is the first step of Love ?

Lord Krishna : Attention on Me who am Love.

Arjuna : If the thoughts of Love flicker and falter in the Yogi's mind—

Lord Krishna : If he fails, you mean—

Arjuna : Yes.

Lord Krishna : No failure ever touches My votaries. Habit masters thought—

Arjuna : And practice perfects Yoga—

Lord Krishna : Repeated concentration on My wisdom, wisdom achieves.

Arjuna : What if habit practice and concentration fail ?

Lord Krishna : If they fail, then My seekers bring their works as sacrifice to My altars wide—

Arjuna : Offerings to my Lord Krishna as candle, incense, wine or bread in the smoke of his temples ?

Lord Krishna : Yes.

Arjuna : What if concentration, sacrifice and work fail ?

Lord Krishna : The desireless work, the renounced deed, the heart from attachments freed, My aspirants lay before My eyes of Grace—

Arjuna : Seeking through Grace perfection ?

Lord Krishna : Yes. For am I not the perfecter ?

Arjuna : What if my deeds fail, renunciation recede and all my vows into ruin break ? What of the absolute failure ?

Lord Krishna : Bring all your failures to My Light ; your renunciation to My Ray ; your vows to Me. I am the grand crematorium whose Radiance burns into ashes all the lapses of the Spirit. (Speaking concisely and deliberately) Know Arjuna that all failures are pauses. All pauses are the steps of concealed releases. All releases are Love.

Arjuna : What is the interregnum of failure ?

Lord Krishna : Evolution's ascending road.

Arjuna : What is the end of evolution ?

Lord Krishna : The eternal progression of Love.

Arjuna : Which is the apex of the climb—Knowledge or Love ?

Lord Krishna : Love.

Arjuna : Why ?

Lord Krishna : What is Knowledge without Love ?

Arjuna : Intellection cold and sight obscure.

Lord Krishna : What is Love without Knowledge ?

Arjuna : Wisdom wide and sight omniscient.

Lord Krishna : Then how can Knowledge outstride Love ?

Arjuna : It cannot.

Lord Krishna : What is the peak of all the Ways ?

Arjuna : Love.

Lord Krishna : What is the highest Yoga ?

Arjuna : Bhakti Yoga. What is to Love nearest in your eyes Lord ?

Lord Krishna : Renunciation.

Arjuna : What are the qualities of the renunciate ?

Lord Krishna : My renunciate lives in Me and I live in him. Governed are his senses; ruled his mind; controlled his being. Even is the tenor of his life. Sorrow and joy mark not the man. Honour or dishonour touch him not. Earth's subtle blandishments move him not. He none disturbs and of none is he disturbed. Compassion is he. Love is he. Such a man I draw to the arbour of My Light lifting him from Samsara's saddened foam.

Arjuna : Such a man loves you and such a man you love ?

Lord Krishna : Such devotees by devotion's road enter My Paradise.

Arjuna : Pleasing God and pleased of God I too tread Devotion's path.

Lord Krishna : Further questions Arjuna ?

Arjuna : No.

Lord Krishna : Then we rise ?

Arjuna : Yes.

(*Arjuna and Lord Krishna lightly withdraw*).

SCENE XIII

THE FIELD AND ITS KNOWER

(On the twelfth day of the battle the Pandavas have advanced within ten miles of the Capital of the Kurus which is now on all sides invested by the forces of Prince Arjuna. The last obstacle is the river whose crossing Lord Krishna is directing. Lord Krishna speaks).

Lord Krishna : Is the river reached ?

Arjuna : Yes, my Lord.

Lord Krishna : And the mine-fields ?

Arjuna : They are breached.

Lord Krishna : On what do you fire ?

Arjuna : On yonder ridge.

Lord Krishna (Grasping the military situation) : And what of the bridge ?

Arjuna (Disappointed) : All the bridges by the Kurus have been destroyed—

Lord Krishna (Correcting) : Save the one bridge where your battalions are employed ?

Arjuna : Yes.

Lord Krishna : Arjuna, what are your orders ?

Arjuna (Alert) : Athwart that one bridge to cross the Kurus' borders.

Lord Krishna : And beyond ?

Arjuna : Beyond the underground shelters of the Duryodhana line we propose to move—

Lord Krishna : Their subterranean tenements to probe and prove?

Arjuna : Yes.

Lord Krishna : Where is the main assault upon the Kurus' ranks?

Arjuna : On the central sector where our tanks have penetrated into the terrain—

Lord Krishna : Of the Kurus' lost domain.

Arjuna : Yes.

Lord Krishna : What of the flanks ?

Arjuna : They have been turned.

Lord Krishna : And the gaps ?

Arjuna : Through the gaps our armies pour into the Kurus' plains.

Lord Krishna : And the fortresses ?

Arjuna : The fortresses of the Duryodhana line have fallen.

Lord Krishna (Hinting the movement) : Whither does your armour drive ?

Arjuna (Sarcastically) : To the Capital of the Kurus with salutations tender—

Lord Krishna (Suggesting the strategy) : The Armistice to proclaim their last surrender—

Arjuna (In anger) : In the Hall of Judgement their crimes secret or open will be tried by my Lord Krishna—

Lord Krishna : The Lord and Judge of all deeds evil or good.

Arjuna : What will be the fate of the chieftains of the Kurus ?

Lord Krishna (Severely) : Death in the lockers of the Chancellery where the plotters plotted against the life of my votary Prince Arjuna.

Arjuna : And what of the territories of the Kurus ?

Lord Krishna : Their territories will be occupied and defended by the arms of the Pandavas—

Arjuna : Ending in Kurukshetra's sacred dust the sound and jar of this premeditated war whose wide alarms have my kingdom shaken and from me taken the peace of subjects who arms abhor and disown.

Lord Krishna : Be assured that My holy Peace will honour the work of your sacred sword.

Arjuna : Then my Lord to themes of Peace may we adjourn—

Lord Krishna (Pointing) : To yonder airy nook—

Arjuna : Beside the rippling brook—

Lord Krishna : Which invites to gentler minstrelsy of thought ?

Arjuna : Yes. May I propound—

Lord Krishna : Propound all your propositions profound of which I shall give you hints Divine.

Arjuna : What is the Field ? Who is the Knower ? What is the Self ? What is the Not-Self ? What are the Strands ?

Lord Krishna : Briefly first I speak. The Field is Maya's domain.

The Knower am I the Paramatma. The Self is Atma.

The Not-Self is the material nature of Man. The Strands are the materials constituents of his being.

Arjuna (Not fully grasping) : My Lord the points enlarge.

Lord Krishna: The Field is Kurukshetra called—Samsara's plain—

Arjuna : Wide Illusion's den where body and mind from birth to birth and death to death play in the deceptive Rings of Maya.

Lord Krishna : Yes.

Arjuna : Wherefore do they play ?

Lord Krishna : For the soul's ultimate release from the world of form—

Arjuna : For emancipation from the hold of Maya?

Lord Krishna : Yes.

Arjuna : Who watches the play ?

Lord Krishna : The Knower of the Field.

Arjuna : Who is the Knower of the Field?

Lord Krishna : I the Paramatma.

Arjuna : Touched or untouched by creation's act ?

Lord Krishna : Unpolluted, stainless, free am I—

Arjuna : By acts untainted ?

Lord Krishna : Yes. Maker of acts, how should I be by act bound ?

Arjuna : Immeasurable Power, you are the Spectator of all actions seeing but not seen by souls ?

Arjuna : Yes. Then what do you survey ?

Lord Krishna : All Maya's high scenario from age to age. For I am the Timeless.

Arjuna : What is the Atma ?

Lord Krishna : The Atma am I.

Arjuna : What is the relationship of the Atma to the Paramatma ?

Lord Krishna : In the Absolute there is no relationship.

Arjuna : The Atma is therefore the Paramatma ?

Lord Krishna : Yes.

Arjuna : What is the Jiva-Atma ?

Lord Krishna : The individual soul.

Arjuna : Then the Jiva-Atma, the Atma and the Paramatma are not distinct ?

Lord Krishna : Because they are One.

Arjuna : What severs them?

Lord Krishna : The lid of Maya.

Arjuna : What unites them ?

Lord Krishna : Nothing. For in essence they are one.

Arjuna : The Jiva-Atma, the Atma, and the Paramatma are the Lords of the Watch ?

Lord Krishna : One Lord of the One Watch.

Arjuna : What divides the Atmas of all souls ?

Lord Krishna : Illusion. In Atma there is no fission.

Arjuna : Therefore the Atmas of all souls is the One Atma ?

Lord Krishna : Yes. I am the one Atma of all souls. I am the Paramatma.

Arjuna : What seemingly divides the Atma.

Lord Krishna : The vision of the Not-Self.

Arjuna : What is the vision of the Not-Self ?

Lord Krishna : Maya.

Arjuna : Who creates the vision of the Not-Self ?

Lord Krishna : The Not-Self.

Arjuna : Then the vision of the Not-Self and the Not-Self are both Maya ?

Lord Krishna : Yes.

Arjuna : Who acts ?

Lord Krishna : The Not-Self.

Arjuna : How does it act ?

Lord Krishna : Through its dreams.

Arjuna : Where does it act ?

Lord Krishna : In the shadows of the land of Maya.

Arjuna : What is the nature of its action ?

Lord Krishna : Maya.

Arjuna : What does not act ?

Lord Krishna : The Atma.

Arjuna : Why does it not act ?

Lord Krishna : Because the Atma is the Real.

Arjuna : What is the action of the Real ?

Lord Krishna : Will.

Arjuna : The Atma is the watcher and not the worker ?

Lord Krishna : Yes.

Arjuna : The Not-Self is the worker and not the watcher ?

Lord Krishna : Yes.

Arjuna : What does the Not-Self the worker weave ?
Lord Krishna : The web of the Illusions.
Arjuna : The Atma is in the body's web enwound ?
Lord Krishna : Yes.
Arjuna : But of the web is free ?
Lord Krishna : Yes.
Arjuna : The net it embraces but of the net it is free ?
Lord Krishna : Like the watchful Spider which is in the web involved but of the web is liberate.
Arjuna : Who is entangled in the web ?
Lord Krishna : The Not-Self.
Arjuna : Why ?
Lord Krishna : Because the Not-Self makes the webs of Maya.
Arjuna : How ?
Lord Krishna : By the Power of the Paramatma.
Arjuna : Through what faculty ?
Lord Krishna : Through its creative faculty of dreams.
Arjuna : What does it dream ?
Lord Krishna : It dreams of the worlds of body and mind—
Arjuna : Which are worlds of Maya ?
Lord Krishna : Yes.
Arjuna : Who is not entangled in the web ?
Lord Krishna : The Atma.
Arjuna : Why ?
Lord Krishna : Because it is the Real.
Arjuna : The Atma is the watcher of the Unreal ?
Lord Krishna : Yes.
Arjuna : Who is the Master of the web ?
Lord Krishna : The Paramatma.
Arjuna : Who is the creator of the Not-Self ?
Lord Krishna : The Paramatma.
Arjuna : Who is the Knower of the web ?
Lord Krishna : The Paramatma.
Arjuna : How does the Paramatma enring the Not-Self ?
Lord Krishna : As tenuous ether which enrings matter gross.
Arjuna : Moving in the womb of matter but by matter untouched ?
Lord Krishna : Yes.
Arjuna : Near and yet far ?

Lord Krishna : Yes.
Arjuna : Boundless and therefore in Bounds ?
Lord Krishna : Yes.
Arjuna : Dwelling in all and therefore dwelling in none ?
Lord Krishna : Yes.
Arjuna : Creator of souls and therefore beyond souls ?
Lord Krishna : Yes.
Arjuna : Master of Forms and therefore Formless ?
Lord Krishna : Yes.
Arjuna : Lord of Motion and therefore Motionless ?
Lord Krishna : Yes.
Arjuna : Sovereign of perception and therefore unperceived ?
Lord Krishna : Yes.
Arjuna : Now to my central query. What is the Not-Self ?
Lord Krishna : The Not-Self is the shadow of the Paramatma.
Arjuna : What is the substance behind the shadow ?
Lord Krishna : The Paramatma.
Arjuna : Who casts the shadow ?
Lord Krishna : The Paramatma.
Arjuna : What is the nature of the shadow ?
Lord Krishna : It is the show and illusion of the Paramatma.
Arjuna : How is the shadow formed ?
Lord Krishna : By the Power of the Maya of the Paramatma.
Arjuna : Is the Power of Maya illusion ?
Lord Krishna : No. The Power of Maya is the Power of the Real. Illusory Power is not Power.
Arjuna : Is the shadow, the creature of Maya, living ?
Lord Krishna : Yes.
Arjuna : What is the criterion of life ?
Lord Krishna : The capacity to create.
Arjuna : Then the Not-Self creates ?
Lord Krishna : Yes.
Arjuna : What does it create ?
Lord Krishna : The Field of Change, Samsara's realms.
Arjuna : What is the veil of the Not-Self ?
Lord Krishna : Corporeality.
Arjuna : What are the gross constituents of the Not-Self ?
Lord Krishna : The gross elements of the body; earth, air, water, fire, the eleven gates of the senses ; the five portals

of smell, touch, taste, form and sound, mind, ego; and the Unmanifest out of perception's range.

Arjuna : What is the ego?

Lord Krishna : The personal self which thinks itself to be the true self of man.

Arjuna : What is mind?

Lord Krishna : The director of the physical action of the ego.

Arjuna : What are the senses?

Lord Krishna : The directed channels of the mind.

Arjuna : What are the five portals of the body?

Lord Krishna : The five receiving centres of the body.

Arjuna : What is the Unmanifest?

Lord Krishna : The Paramatma behind all manifestations.

Arjuna : What is the support of the Not-Self behind the veils?

Lord Krishna : The Paramatma.

Arjuna : What is the field of the Not-Self?

Lord Krishna : The field of body and mind.

Arjuna : Who is the possessor of the body and mind of the Not-Self behind the veils?

Lord Krishna : The Jiva-Atma.

Arjuna : What is the Jiva-Atma?

Lord Krishna : The Individual Soul.

Arjuna : What are the vestures of the Jiva-Atma?

Lord Krishna : The body and mind of the Not-Self.

Arjuna : What are the fields of the Atma?

Lord Krishna : The limitless fields of the Paramatma.

Arjuna : Whence proceed the Not-Self and the Atma?

Lord Krishna : From the Paramatma.

Arjuna : The Paramatma has no beginning and no ending?

Lord Krishna : No.

Arjuna : Then the Not-Self and the Atma also have neither beginning nor ending?

Lord Krishna : No. They move in the cycles of Eternity.

Arjuna : What are the Strands of the Not-Self which bind the soul to the rounds of Samsara?

Lord Krishna : First is the Strand of the Asuric Forces, Tamas, or darkness which imprisons the Jiva in the halls of the Illusions. The second is the Strand of the vital Force of desire or Rajas which keeps the Jiva in the bonds of the cravings. Third is the Force of Purity, Sattwa, which moves the Jiva out of the shows of Maya.

Arjuna : Do the three Strands appertain to the Atma ?

Lord Krishna : No. The Atma does not reside in the world of Illusions.

Arjuna : The Atma is the spectator of the show ?

Lord Krishna : Yes.

Arjuna : How is the release from the Not-Self achieved by your Yogis ?

Lord Krishna : By many ways. My aspirants come to Me by many roads. Some by meditation ; some by abstract philosophies; some by holy lives ; some by holy works; and some by the teachings of My Gurus embrace My Light. He who knows the fields of the Not-Self; the Atma as the watcher of the field; the Paramatma as the Knower of the field; and the three Strands as the constituents of the field has the supreme release.

Arjuna : Through action on Kurukshetra's sacred plain give me the supreme release.

Lord Krishna (Beaming with benevolence) : I will give.

(*Exeunt Arjuna and Lord Krishna*).

SCENE XIV

THE TRIPLE STRANDS OF THE NOT-SELF

(On the thirteenth day of the battle, Lord Krishna is looking at the banner of the Kurus—still flying defiantly over their Capital. Prince Arjuna speaks giving his last reportings of the "Operation Battle—Axe").

Arjuna (Joyously) : My Lord, we have crossed the river !

Lord Krishna : Don't halt. Pursue the Kurus beyond the shiver of the waters till their last buildings quiver in the shower of your bombs aerial—

Arjuna : I will.

Lord Krishna : What of your tread-way ?

Arjuna : All our bridges, pontoons and skiffs are stretched along the curves of this river—

Lord Krishna (Keenly viewing the scene) : At the bend I see no bridge—

Arjuna : There my Lord our tread-ways end.

Lord Krishna : How stand the Kurus' Aerodromes ? Surrounded ?

Arjuna : By our paratroops encompassed and impounded.

Lord Krishna : Where are the Kurus planes ?

Arjuna : Our skies are clear. On the aerial roadway their wings are grounded.

Lord Krishna : And the planes of the Pandavas ?

Arjuna : They sweep the proud terrain overflooded—

Lord Krishna : Overflooded ?

Arjuna : Yes. My Lord, we have hit the dams—

Lord Krishna : Whose sluices spill all along the river-bed a masterly show of ruining waters—

Arjuna : Soon shall all the sons and daughters of the Kurus be drenched with the dew of tears—

Lord Krishna (Sarcastically) : Damping their enthusiasm for war unprovoked in the shelters of the Chancellery—

Arjuna (Gazing at the flag on the roof of the Chancellery) : Why flutters that flag so ?

Lord Krishna : That's evil's very sign and doom now drooping in the loud din of war. Fire upon it. Blast the flag ! Haul downths banner of the lords of darkness ! Plant upon it the banner of the Four Freedoms.

Arjuna : My Lord we will.

Lord Krishna : Issue directives, Encircle the Capitoleum. Fire the city of the Kurus. Spare none. Race to the Chancellery.

Arjuna (In urgent call) : Guards !

Guards : We are here.

Arjuna : Summon the courier.

Guards (As the courier enters) : He is here.

Arjuna (To the courier) : Despatch in cipher this signal to the heads of all commands : "All armour must race to the Chancellery. Allies and Confederates of the Pandavas. We join you in the halls of the Chancellery. Haul down the banner of Duryodhana."

Courier : My Lord, the signal will be despatched without delay.

Arjuna (To Lord Krishna) : My Lord, shall we to the portico ?

Lord Krishna (Smiling) : For your last interrogatories ?

Arjuna : Yes.

Lord Krishna : Well then interrogate.

Arjuna : How is the Not-Self born ?

Lord Krishna : By the union of the immortal Atma and its shadow the Not-Self.

Arjuna : Who fructifies the union ?

Lord Krishna : Brahma.

Arjuna : Who is the seed ?

Lord Krishna : Brahma.

Arjuna : Who is the Sire ?

Lord Krishna : Brahma.

Arjuna : Where is its womb ?

Lord Krishna : In Brahma.

Arjuna : By whom is it dissolved ?

Lord Krishna : By Brahma.

Arjuna : By whom is it brought to birth again ?

Lord Krishna : By Brahma.

Arjuna : How is the Not-Self bound ?

Lord Krishna : By the triple Strands of the Not-Self.

Arjuna : What is the first thread of the Not-Self?

Lord Krishna : Purity or Sattwa.

Arjuna : What is the second ?

Lord Krishna : Passion or Rajas.

Arjuna : What is the third ?

Lord Krishna : Delusion or Tamas.

Arjuna : The three knots of ignorance bind the embodied Jiva in the House of Matter ?

Lord Krishna : Yes.

Arjuna : What does Purity breed ?

Lord Krishna : Virtue.

Arjuna : What does Virtue breed ?

Lord Krishna : Freedom.

Arjuna : Then Purity is the first release ?

Lord Krishna : Yes.

Arjuna : What does Passion breed ?

Lord Krishna : Desire.

Arjuna : What from desire springs ?

Lord Krishna : Cravings for the fields of the illusions.

Arjuna : Passion then is the first bondage ?

Lord Krishna : Yes.

Arjuna : What does Delusion breed ?

Lord Krishna : The field of the delusions—Maya.

Arjuna : Delusion is the next bondage ?

Lord Krishna : Yes.

Arjuna : Does Purity transcend Good and Evil ?

Lord Krishna : No.

Arjuna : Purity is then bound in the fields of Good and Evil ?

Lord Krishna : Yes.

Arjuna : Good and Evil work in the fields of the illusions ?

Lord Krishna : Yes.

Arjuna : Purity works within the limits of the illusions ?

Lord Krishna : Yes.

Arjuna : Purity then both binds and frees ?

Lord Krishna : Yes.

Arjuna : To what does Purity lead ?

Lord Krishna : To greed, lust and anger—

Arjuna : Which are the portals of Hell?

Lord Krishna : Yes.

Arjuna : To what does Delusion lead?

Lord Krishna : To the roads of Samsara.

Arjuna : What is the fruit of Purity?

Lord Krishna : Bliss.

Arjuna : And of Passion?

Lord Krishna : Pain.

Arjuna : And of Delusion?

Lord Krishna : Rebirth in wombs of defilement.

Arjuna : From the last swoon of life, whither does the man of Purity go?

Lord Krishna : To the opening doors of my secret heavens.

Arjuna : And the man of Passion?

Lord Krishna : To the fields of the illusions birth after birth for the cleansing of the passions.

Arjuna: And the man of delusion?

Lord Krishna : To rebirth in the realms of Samsara—

Arjuna : For what?

Lord Krishna : For regeneration from the sleep of nescience.

Arjuna : How does man cross the three threads of the Not-Self?

Lord Krishna : By releases.

Arjuna : What is the release from the first thread of the Not-Self?

Lord Krishna : Release from Virtue.

Arjuna : What is the release from Virtue?

Lord Krishna : Release from the pair of opposites—Good and Evil.

Arjuna : By the transcendence of Good and Evil?

Lord Krishna : Yes.

Arjuna : What does the release from Virtue bring?

Lord Krishna : The freedom of the Absolute.

Arjuna : What is the goal of Purity?

Lord Krishna : The Paramatma.

Arjuna : What are Good and Evil in the shine of the Paramatma?

Lord Krishna : The shadows of Samsara.

Arjuna : What is release from the second thread of the Not-Self?

Lord Krishna : Release from the Passions?

Arjuna : What does the release from the Passions bring?

Lord Krishna : The Bliss of the Absolute.

Arjuna : What is the release from the third thread of the Not-Self?

Lord Krishna : The release from the fields of the delusions.

Arjuna : What does the release from the fields of the illusions bring?

Lord Krishna : The Vision of the Absolute.

Arjuna : What of the man who has crossed the triple Strands of the Not-Self?

Lord Krishna : He is my liberate Yogi—the Jiva-Mukti.

Arjuna : In him all the threads of the Not-Self are transformed?

Lord Krishna : Yes.

Arjuna : Into what is Purity transformed?

Lord Krishna : Into Bliss.

Arjuna : Into what is Passion transformed?

Lord Krishna : Into Absolute Existence.

Arjuna : Into what is Delusion transformed?

Lord Krishna : Into Absolute Light.

Arjuna : In crossing the three threads of the Strands, what does your liberate Yogi attain?

Lord Krishna : Absolute Bliss, Absolute Existence, Absolute Light.

Arjuna : What are the qualities of your Jiva-Mukti?

Lord Krishna : My Jiva-Mukti in the flesh is wide awake. He has by austerities crossed Samsara's illusory rounds. He has passed the fields of the attachments. He has moved beyond the pair of the opposites—Good and Evil. The outer life of mind and body does not obsess or obstruct his tranquility. For he dwells in the inner Existence of My silent heavens.

Arjuna : My Lord make me in this life your Jiva-Mukti—

Lord Krishna : I do. Rise to My holy ascensions through work in Kurukshetra's field.

Arjuna : I rise.

(*Exeunt Arjuna and Lord Krishna*).

SCENE XV

THE SUPREME DIVINE

(*On the fourteenth day of the battle at midnight Lord Krishna and Arjuna are watching the bombardment of the Capital of the Kurus when Arjuna speaks*).

Arjuna : My Lord we are in the suburbs of the Kurus city—

Lord Krishna : I know.

Arjuna : Do you see the distant glow which enwraps the spire of the Capitoleum with the holocaust of the fire of our arms ?

Lord Krishna : Yes.

Arjuna (Tearfully) : Warm are the streets of the Kurus, fallen their buildings, and desolate their homes. How by the ire of our bombs is their fair city lit !

Lord Krishna : O Arjuna of the gentle lid, the pity of it, the pity of it !

Arjuna : Yet the predestined play must proceed from scene to scene and act to act till the curtains of the imperial drama fall majestical in the vestibule and the hall of the Chancellery of the Kurus !

Lord Krishna : Yes.

Arjuna : While the metropolis of the Kurus burns in the flames of war, shall we by this tree rest—

Lord Krishna : Reviving in the pause of battle the sweet ideations of My ancient Wisdom—

Arjuna : Yes.

Lord Krishna : What would you hear ?

Arjuna : A myth.

Lord Krishna : Then I shall explain to you the myth of My Aswattha Tree with roots below and roots above.

Arjuna : How does the Aswattha Tree grow ?

Lord Krishna : From the roots below.

Arjuna : What are the roots below ?

Lord Krishna : The roots below are the roots of the Absolute whose mystic secret none may know.

Arjuna : What do the roots below do ?

Lord Krishna : They push into being the leaves, branches, and roots above.

Arjuna : What are the leaves above ?

Lord Krishna : Songs of the Vedas in Samsara's realms.

Arjuna : What are the branches above ?

Lord Krishna : The organs of the senses in Samsara's field.

Arjuna : What are the roots above ?

Lord Krishna : The roots of rebirth in Samsara's Rounds.

Arjuna : What is the sap in the Tree above ?

Lord Krishna : The three Strands of the Not-Self.

Arjuna : What is the Tree above ?

Lord Krishna : The Tree of the Not-Self.

Arjuna : What is the Tree of the Not-Self ?

Lord Krishna : Samsara's broad terrain.

Arjuna : When the Tree of the Not-Self dies, what procreates ?

Lord Krishna : The Paramatma.

Arjuna : How ?

Lord Krishna : The roots of the Tree above return to the roots of the Absolute below for regeneration.

Arjuna : In your roots below where are Samsara's Show ?

Lord Krishna : In My roots below Samsara's Shows are closed.

Arjuna : Whence again begins Maya's rule ?

Lord Krishna : My roots below start afresh the Shows of Maya's charms.

Arjuna : From birth to birth and death to death in the cycles of Eternity ?

Lord Krishna : Yes.

Arjuna : So fresh leaves, fresh branches, and fresh roots spring forth above from time to time on Maya's floor ?

Lord Krishna : Yes.

Arjuna : What is the Tree of the Not-Self which is born again and again ?

Lord Krishna : The Tree of the Not-Self is an aspect of My great Illusion.

Arjuna : What are the roots of the Absolute below which are not born again and again.

Lord Krishna : They are the roots of the Absolute Substance from which Eternal Regeneration proceeds. How can they die ?

Arjuna : Then the roots above and the roots below are both the roots of the Paramatma ?

Lord Krishna : Yes, for the Paramatma is the All.

Arjuna : How do souls cut the Tree of Samsara ?

Lord Krishna : By the keen axe of detachment.

Arjuna : What is the keen axe of detachment the symbol of?

Lord Krishna : It is the symbol of the Universal Fire ?

Arjuna : What does the Divine Fire do ?

Lord Krishna : It burns into cinders the leaves, the branches, and the roots of the Samsara Tree.

Arjuna : Then souls who by the axe of detachment cleave the Tree of dreams, cannot return to earth as their roots of Illusion are dead ?

Lord Krishna : They pass from the earth field and are free of Samsara's reign.

Arjuna : For such no duty remains to be done in the rounds of the dust ?

Lord Krishna : No.

Arjuna : Where do such souls go ?

Lord Krishna : To the planes of the Paramatma—

Arjuna : Where neither the light of the moon, nor the light of the star nor the light of the sun shine—

Lord Krishna : For the Hall of the Paramatma is itself Light.

Arjuna : Does progression in the fields of the Paramatma halt ?

Lord Krishna : No. Life progresses from eternity to eternity.

Arjuna : How do your royal Rishis see you, Lord ?

Lord Krishna : In three levels of perception. In the first level they see Me as the Lord of the Not-Self, Master of Samsara, in the mutable fields of My manifestations.

Arjuna : Present in mind and in the five senses ?

Lord Krishna : Yes.

Arjuna : Embodied in the sun and moon and the stars—

Lord Krishna : Yes.

Arjuna : The subtle life behind all phenomena ?

Lord Krishna : Yes.

Arjuna : Who perceives your sensitive Omnipresence in Samsara ?

Lord Krishna : My disciplined Yogi.

Arjuna : How does he perceive you ?

Lord Krishna : Through the spiritual perception.

Arjuna : How does he attain spiritual perception ?

Lord Krishna : Through My releases.

Arjuna : Who does not perceive you behind Samsara's veils ?

Lord Krishna : The man of delusion.

Arjuna : What does he perceive ?

Lord Krishna : Delusion.

Arjuna : In the second level of perception, what do your Sages see ?

Lord Krishna : They see Me as the changeless Atma.

Arjuna : What is the changeless Atma ?

Lord Krishna : The Imperishable Self of all—

Arjuna : Beyond manifestation—

Lord Krishna : Yes.

Arjuna : Where is it seated in the flesh ?

Lord Krishna : In the heart.

Arjuna : What proceed from the Atma ?

Lord Krishna : My memories of past births, My Knowledge, My Vedas.

Arjuna : How is the Atma perceived ?

Lord Krishna : By the Atmic perception of My Rishis.

Arjuna : How is the Atmic perception attained ?

Lord Krishna : By My Atmic releases.

Arjuna : In the third level of perception, what do your Yogis see ?

Lord Krishna : The Supreme Divine Spirit beyond the Not-Self and the Self.

Arjuna : Who is the last person of this trinity of perceptions ?

Lord Krishna : I the Paramatma.

Arjuna : How is the Paramatma perceived ?

Lord Krishna : By the releases of the Paramatma.

Arjuna : How is this trinity of perceptions dissolved ?

Lord Krishna : By the Vision of the Paramatma.

Arjuna : How does the Spirit Divine play in the shadows of Samsara ?

Lord Krishna : As a subtle wind aerial it blows unseen in all My vineyards. It slips into the stone. It slides into the plant.

It breathes into the twin nostrils of man. My rare wind gathers viewless all the scents and smells of the earth. For I am the Aroma and Wine divine.

Arjuna (Smilingly) : Then give me Lord the sip of your scented nectar from the cup of all your perfumes sweet.

Lord Krishna (With glancing eyes) : I will. Arjuna, your lids are heavy ?

Arjuna : Yes, Lord.

Lord Krishna : Then let us rise.

Arjuna (Anticipating the end of the battle) : To-morrow may perchance be the end of our grand emprise.

Lord Krishna : Perchance.

(*Exeunt Arjuna and Lord Krishna*).

SCENE XVI

THE DIVINE AND THE UNDIVINE

(*On the fifteenth day of the battle Arjuna and Lord Krishna in the imperial tent are playing chess. The ambassadors of the Kurus have crossed the lines for presenting the terms of a truce preparatory to their unconditional surrender*).

Arjuna (Hearing a noise) : What noise stirs about our royal tents ? Guards, come forward from your hidden battlements.

Guards : We are here my Lord.

Arjuna : What's the row about ?

Guards : The Kurus have crossed the lines.

Arjuna (Surprised) : For attack ?

Guards (Smiling) : No, for parley ?

Arjuna (In anger) : Who invited them to our imperial presence ? They disturb our game.

Guards : They sneaked across the grass carrying the white flag of general surrender.

Arjuna : Why did you allow them to pass ?

Guards : They eluded the vigil of the mass of our troops—

Arjuna : Did you not molest them ?

Guards : No, they moved unmarked.

Arjuna : Did you not arrest them ?

Guards (Smiling) : They walked too fast—but we halted them at your tent to hear from you my Lord their fate. What are your orders ?

Arjuna (In an imperial voice) : Tell them to wait. My Lord Krishna and I play chess.

Guards : Yes, we will.

Lord Krishna (As the guards withdraw) : It is your move, Arjuna.

Arjuna (Moving a chess piece) : There.

Lord Krishna (Smilingly) : Thanks, I take your Bishop—

Arjuna : There !

Lord Krishna : Thanks again. There goes your Knight—

Arjuna : There !

Lord Krishna : There you lose your Castle—

Arjuna (Failing but merry) : Tut. Tut.

Lord Krishna : Beware. Your Queen is in danger.

Arjuna : My Lord's moves are keen—

Lord Krishna (Understanding the innuendo of his disciple) : I say once more. In danger is your Queen.

Arjuna (Also understanding the hint) : You pursue your votaries too swift.

Lord Krishna (Laughing) : Look to the shift of your pawns.

Arjuna : My Lord my Queen is taken.

Lord Krishna (Checkmating Arjuna) : Now where do you move ?

Arjuna : If I am not mistaken, my game is up. You my Lord have won.

Lord Krishna (Hinting) : My wisdom always wins.

Arjuna (Thinking of the game of life) : My Lord Krishna, you play. I play. Your play succeeds.

Lord Krishna (Comforting) : No, I but chaff. You have won the game (Pointing to the Guards). Look to the war news Arjuna—

Guards (Entering) : Dramatic developments—

Arjuna : What developments ?

Guards : The Chancellery is all but taken. The Kurus on all fronts have surrendered.

Lord Krishna (Directing Arjuna) : Let the Plenipotentiaries of the Kurus come in—

Arjuna : Our royal presence will wait—

Guards : My Lord here are the Plenipotentiaries—

Arjuna (Coldly to the Kurus as they enter) : What is your mission ?

Plenipotentiaries : Peace.

Arjuna : Where are your credentials?

Plenipotentiaries : We have none.

Arjuna (Sternly) : Because all vestiges of an accredited Government are gone. Where is Duryodhana's authority ?

Plenipotentiaries : He has none. His authority is disowned by his people. The dictator of the Kurus has fallen my Lord.

Arjuna : Where is Duryodhana ?

Plenipotentiaries : In his bunker moving imaginary armies in his map room.

Arjuna : Poor planning I deem. Tell him that we shall pursue him to the bunker alive or dead. (Speaking menacingly) Now Gentlemen, as you are not accredited representatives of any Government, retire. (Again looking severely) In twenty minutes we open fire.

Lord Krishna (Approvingly) : Well done Arjuna.

Arjuna : A diplomatic rebuff, my Lord ! The Kurus tell us that war is the continuation of diplomacies.

Lord Krishna : Let your arms show them that diplomacy is the continuation of war !

Arjuna : But my brows are bent upon thoughts of peace—

Lord Krishna (Catching the hint) : Then why not resume your dialogues of delight which from wisdom proceeds ?

Arjuna (Indicating a seat) : Shall we sit here ?

Lord Krishna : Yes. Well, go on with your questions—

Arjuna : Tell me of the man divine and the man undivine. What are their paths ? What their work ? What their doom ?

Lord Krishna : The sign of the man divine is austerity and wisdom. The holy path he seeks. The holy work he pursues. The holy release he wins. His soul is in Me and My soul is in him. For birthlessness and deathlessness he strives.

Arjuna : What does he achieve ?

Lord Krishna : Freedom from birth and death in the hidden meadows of My Paradise. Such men I deem the sons of wisdom on the subtle arc of the ascent to Me.

Arjuna : And the man undivine ?

Lord Krishna : The man undivine is on the arc of the descent on a path which from Me recedes. From Me he rebels. From Me he withdraws. His friend is, Satan, the dark angel of unwisdom and error.

Arjuna : Where does Lucifer entice him ?

Lord Krishna : To the first portal of hell.

Arjuna : What does he find there ?

Lord Krishna : The demon of desire.

Arjuna : How does desire move ?

Lord Krishna : With subtle tentacles of grasp and grip.

Arjuna : As the marine monster, the Spider of the Deep—

Lord Krishna : The many-mouthed Octopus spilling in the ocean's coze the purpureal poison—

Arjuna : In whose bad wash souls spin in the round of the eternities. How does the Spider of the seas close upon its prey?

Lord Krishna : With a thousand hands it sucks its victim into the belly of the nether air where no light is and where all souls sigh—

Arjuna : Into the sulphurous fumes of the lowest hell?

Lord Krishna : Yes.

Arjuna : And the next step?

Lord Krishna : The subtle Siren of the slippery kiss summons the sluggard to the second portal of hell—

Arjuna (Anticipating) : O God!

Lord Krishna : To the sensuous sheets of lust!

Arjuna : O horrid broth brewed in the densest dens of the Asuras!

Lord Krishna : Fit broth for the devilish estate of the perjured man undivine!

Arjuna : How does the Sylph of lust proceed with the sensuous kiss?

Lord Krishna : Her sensuous shape she strips for the eyes of waste.

Arjuna : And with coil upon serpentining coil in rigorous grip she slips amorous about the languorous lips of loveless love—

Lord Krishna : Crushing the body and killing the soul—

Arjuna : Despoiling the man of his high divinity with deep dark injuries to the unsatisfied longings of the weeping flesh?

Lord Krishna : Yes.

Arjuna : How does the amorous Python go to her couch and kill?

Lord Krishna : With an uncoiling hiss releasing the kiss she drives the laggard to the lowest slime of the vexed Limbo.

Arjuna : And next?

Lord Krishna : The raven wing of wrath blacker than the black blizzard of the Arctic cold hales the fool body and limb to the third portal of hell.

Arjuna : What does black anger do?

Lord Krishna : It opens wide the lids of Pandora's casket from which all the demons of the Limbo fly to the throat of the man undivine.

Arjuna : Pushing him into the furthest vaults of hell.

Lord Krishna : Yes.

Arjuna : What is the end of the works of the man undivine ?

Lord Krishna : Death and birth and birth and death in Maya's cyclic rounds.

Arjuna : What is the end of the works of the man divine ?

Lord Krishna : Bliss in the seventh heaven.

Arjuna : What is at the end of the arc of the descent of the sons of folly ?

Lord Krishna : Beyond hell's last border is My Light.

Arjuna : Then what happens to the sons of folly at the last edge of darkness ?

Lord Krishna : Them I push into My Light.

Arjuna : Where Lord is your deepest Power ?

Lord Krishna : Among the denizens of the Limbo.

Arjuna : Why ?

Lord Krishna : How can salvation come to My sons of folly in hell's deepest caves save by the exercise of My deepest Power ?

Arjuna : The worst sin needs the first Light.

Lord Krishna : I am the lordly hound of the chase —

Arjuna : And your feet are swiftest in following the sons of folly ?

Lord Krishna : Yes.

Arjuna : What if, my Lord, the sons of folly elude your pursuit ?

Lord Krishna (Smiling) : My Arjuna, who can elude the Absolute ?

Arjuna : Then all the sons of folly reach the Light ?

Lord Krishna : Yes.

Arjuna : By perfecting through repeated births ?

Lord Krishna : Yes.

Arjuna : What is at the top of the arc of the ascent of your sons of wisdom ?

Lord Krishna : My Light.

Arjuna : The same Light which your saved sons of folly reach ?

Lord Krishna : Yes. For My Light is One.

Arjuna : Then all the sons of folly and all the sons of wisdom meet in your Light ?

Lord Krishna : Yes.

Arjuna : Then the arc of the descent and the arc of the ascent join ?

Lord Krishna : Yes.

Arjuna : Where is the perfect Circle ?

Lord Krishna : In My covered heaven.

Arjuna : Where is the perfect bow ?

Lord Krishna : In My veiled skies.

Arjuna : My Lord show me the perfect Circle and the perfect Bow.

Lord Krishna : I will.

Arjuna : War's cares upon me press.

Lord Krishna : So let us retire from this sweet recess.

Arjuna : Yes.

(*Exeunt Arjuna and Lord Krishna*).

SCENE XVII

THE THREEFOLD FAITH

(On the sixteenth day of the battle, Arjuna and Lord Krishna are watching from a short distance the conflagration in the Capital of the Kurus).

Arjuna (Ruefully) : My Lord, how are the mighty fallen! How are the high places of the Kurus broken! How the imperial palaces of their Chancellery, once the repository of Power and the unholy hall of the wide-ranging armouries of the world, under the moan and groan of our bombs, blaze and burn!

Lord Krishna : Let them burn. From those flames the lords of the Kurus have yet to learn the necessary truths of My immemorial wisdom which all territorial aggrandisement and the bad race of international arms forbids and annuls.

Arjuna : Yet Lord my heart is full of tears and my eyes of ruth.

Lord Krishna (Firmly) : Shed not one tear for the destruction of the Kurus. Pursue truth and not ruth. Remember in war resolution and in defeat defiance—

Arjuna : And in peace magnanimity—

Lord Krishna : Magnanimity in peace without wisdom is error.

Arjuna : What should I search in peace?

Lord Krishna : Good-will in peace. Goodwill.

Arjuna : But what of this destruction which moves apace from hour to hour in the public squares of the Chancellery?

Lord Krishna : Destruction, Arjuna, is renewal.

Arjuna : What will my Lord renew?

Lord Krishna : The new race of the Kurus disciplined by virtue and not by arms.

Arjuna : And what of these buildings?

Lord Krishna : From their rubble new buildings will rise—

Arjuna : Nobler mansions of virtuous men—

Lord Krishna : Seeking in peace a paradise of marts—

Arjuna : Advanced by the arts of the new Sciences—

Lord Krishna : Bringing commercial prosperity to the lands of the Kurus and the Pandavas united in the single kingdom of my Prince Arjuna—

Arjuna : And what of their Capital ?

Lord Krishna : It shall not be denied renewal. From its cinders will spring the new Capital of the Kurus—

Lord Krishna : Dedicated to the Temple of Peace—

Arjuna : Abjuring the ways of war ?

Lord Krishna : Yes.

Arjuna : And what of my subjects ?

Lord Krishna : The Kurus and the Pandavas will render allegiance to the one Crown of the kingdom of Prince Arjuna !

Arjuna : May your prophecies be true !

Lord Krishna : I am the Prophecy and the Truth !

Arjuna : Now my Lord—

Lord Krishna (Catching the hint) : You spy the bower of thymes and jasmins—

Arjuna : Where we may spend the last hour of your discourses.

Lord Krishna (Moving to the bower) : Well, then pursue your theme.

Arjuna (Sitting with Lord Krishna in the bower) : Now my Lord I have grasped the breadth and circumference of your teachings. I would address my questions to the periphery of your wisdom.

Lord Krishna : Do.

Arjuna : Tell me Lord what are the threefold forms of Faith ? How do they relate to our Scriptures, to our Rites, to our Worship, Sacrifices, Austerities, and our Charities ?

Lord Krishna : Very well. I shall deal with them point by point. Arjuna, what do you see at dayrise ?

Arjuna : Light.

Lord Krishna : And at day-fall ?

Arjuna : Twilight.

Lord Krishna : And at night ?

Arjuna : Darkness.

Lord Krishna : Are these not the gradations of the sun ?

Arjuna : Yes.

Lord Krishna : Then know that in all Faith there are like gradations.

Arjuna : What is the first Faith ?

Lord Krishna : The Faith of Purity.

Arjuna : What is the Faith of Purity ?

Lord Krishna : The Faith of the Sattwic man.

Arjuna : What does the man of virtue see ?

Lord Krishna : The seven Rays of the transcendental Light.

Arjuna : Is the man of virtue fully illumined ?

Lord Krishna : Yes.

Arjuna : He has illumined Knowledge, Wisdom, and Vision occult ?

Lord Krishna : Yes.

Arjuna : Then the first Faith is illumined Knowledge, Wisdom, and Vision occult ?

Lord Krishna : Yes.

Arjuna : What is the second Faith ?

Lord Krishna : The Faith of Passion.

Arjuna : What does the Rajas man see ?

Lord Krishna : The world of Maya in the twilight of the passions.

Arjuna : He therefore gropes in the worlds of desire ?

Lord Krishna : Yes.

Arjuna : His footsteps falter in the twilight ?

Lord Krishna : Yes.

Arjuna : Then the second Faith is not illumined Knowledge but doubt ?

Lord Krishna : Yes.

Arjuna : What is the third Faith ?

Lord Krishna : The Faith of the deluded man.

Arjuna : What does the Tamas soul see ?

Lord Krishna : Maya.

Arjuna : What is the Faith of Maya ?

Lord Krishna : No Faith at all but delusion.

Arjuna : Then the third Faith is not doubt but darkness ?

Lord Krishna : For the Tamas soul dwells in night.

Arjuna : The first Faith is of the daylight ?

Lord Krishna : Yes.

Arjuna : The second Faith of the twilight ?

Lord Krishna : Yes.

Arjuna : The third Faith is of night ?

Lord Krishna : Yes.

Arjuna : What is the Sattwic sight ?

Lord Krishna : The vision of Light.

Arjuna : What is the Rajas sight ?

Lord Krishna : The vision of twilight.
Arjuna : What is the Tamas sight ?
Lord Krishna : The vision of night.
Arjuna : Is the vision of night Maya ?
Lord Krishna : Yes.
Arjuna : Then the Tamas sight is not sight ?
Lord Krishna : No, for it is blindness.
Arjuna : What is the fruit of the Sattwic Faith ?
Lord Krishna : Light.
Arjuna : What is the fruit of the Rajas and Tamas Faiths ?
Lord Krishna : The round of births in Maya's rings.
Arjuna : What does the Sattwic Faith work for ?
Lord Krishna : For works without fruits.
Arjuna : What does the Rajas Faith work for ?
Lord Krishna : For the fruits of desire.
Arjuna : What does the Tamas Faith work for ?
Lord Krishna : For the self of the deluded ego.
Arjuna : Its works are therefore illusion?
Lord Krishna : Yes.
Arjuna : What does the deluded ego attain ?
Lord Krishna : Nothing. Its works are vain.
Arjuna : What do the Rajas and Tamas Faiths effect ?
Lord Krishna : Bondages for the soul.
Arjuna : What does the Sattwic Faith effect ?
Lord Krishna : Liberation from the rounds of Maya.
Arjuna : What is Holy Scripture ?
Lord Krishna : My revealed Word preparatory to My unrevealed visions.
Arjuna : Addressed to whom ?
Lord Krishna : To all races, persons, and creeds.
Arjuna : To the brotherhood of the human race ?
Lord Krishna : To the brotherhood of souls who form the brotherhood of the human race.
Arjuna : Then your Holy Scripture is the Universal Scripture of the brotherhood of human souls ?
Lord Krishna : Yes.
Arjuna : What of him who your Scripture disobeys ?
Lord Krishna : Him My Asuras follow with the Book of the Divided Creeds.

Arjuna : Then all Scriptures are to be obeyed ?

Lord Krishna : For they carry the canons and commandments of the Universal Lord.

Arjuna : What of those who your Scriptures deny but with pure heart affirm the deed of purity ?

Lord Krishna : Their deeds of purity I accept but their denial of the Scriptures I reject.

Arjuna : How do you correct.

Lord Krishna : By repeated births I turn them back to My Scriptures—

Arjuna : Till they affirm the faith of the Scriptures ?

Lord Krishna : Yes.

Arjuna : How do you chastise the deniers of the Scriptures ?

Lord Krishna : By the pain of repeated births.

Arjuna : What is the relationship of the threefold Faiths to the Scriptures ?

Lord Krishna : The Sattwic man sees in the Scriptures Light.

Arjuna : What does the Rajas man see in the Scriptures ?

Lord Krishna : Doubt.

Arjuna : And the Tamas man ?

Lord Krishna : He is the creature of rebellion—

Arjuna : The outcast of heaven, the inmate of hell, he sees nothing. For he repudiates the Scriptures ?

Lord Krishna : Yes.

Arjuna : What are the Holy Rites ?

Lord Krishna : The handmaid of the Scriptures.

Arjuna : The necessary staff of all creeds ?

Lord Krishna : Yes.

Arjuna : Who alone may abandon the staff of the creeds ?

Lord Krishna : Only My surrendered Rishis.

Arjuna : Why ?

Lord Krishna : My surrendered Rishis need not the staff of the creeds. They are in the Holy Light.

Arjuna : What is the relationship of Food to the threefold Faith ?

Lord Krishna : The Food of the Sattwic man is light, pure, and from acidity and pungency free.

Arjuna : And the Food of the Rajas man ?

Lord Krishna : His Food is acrid provoking the passions.

Arjuna : And the Food of the Tamas man ?

Lord Krishna : The Food of the Tamas is bad and bitter pleasurable to the tongue but death to the Spirit—

Arjuna : What is the relationship of the three Sacrifices to the threefold Faiths ?

Lord Krishna : The Sacrifice of the Sattwic man gives release. For it is the offering of the pure heart free of desire.

Arjuna : And the Sacrifice of the Rajas man ?

Lord Krishna : It is show.

Arjuna : What is beneath the show ?

Lord Krishna : The hand of desire.

Arjuna : Does it bind or release ?

Lord Krishna : It binds.

Arjuna : What is the Sacrifice of the Tamas man ?

Lord Krishna : Illusion.

Arjuna : What does he seek in the Sacrifice ?

Lord Krishna : The darkness of his own desires.

Arjuna : His Sacrifice is selfishness and not Sacrifice ?

Lord Krishna : Yes.

Arjuna : The Sacrifice of the Sattwic man is purity, the Sacrifice of the Rajas man impurity, and the Sacrifice of the Tamas man is no Sacrifice at all ?

Lord Krishna : Yes.

Arjuna : What are the three austerities of the Faith ?

Lord Krishna : The austerities of body, speech, and mind.

Arjuna : What are the austerities of the body ?

Lord Krishna : Penances and postures in the holy shrine.

Arjuna : And austerities of speech ?

Lord Krishna : Silence in temple and shrine.

Arjuna : And the austerities of mind ?

Lord Krishna : Meditation and Remembrance of My Name in temple or shrine.

Arjuna : What are the three Charities of the Faith ?

Lord Krishna : The Charities of the Sattwic man is marked by measured wisdom and is free of wanton waste. For he gives at the right time, the right place, and to the right persons, his gifts without thought of reward. When he seems to take, most he gives. His denials are silent gifts.

(Looking at Arjuna occultly) Arjuna are you falling into sleep ?

Arjuna (Awakening from trance induced by Lord Krishna) : No, my Lord, I do not doze.

Lord Krishna (Stimulating with his light secretly) : Are you sure ?

Arjuna (Protesting) : My honoured Lord, I attend.

Lord Krishna : Your eyes are shut !

Arjuna : But my soul is awake.

Lord Krishna : Then I proceed. The Charity of the Sattwic man is rich with the opulences of the Spirit. Not so the Charities of the Rajas man. His Charities are subtle withdrawals. Desires strike the outstretched hand of help. His givings are secret takings. For his impassioned self is held in the vice of greed. (Deliberately inducing trance in Arjuna) Arjuna, heed !

Arjuna (Protesting) : My Lord, my lids do not doze. I hear.

Lord Krishna (Continuing) : Otherwise is the Charity of the Tamas man. He is the fool. His philanthropies are the covers of the hypocrite. Indiscriminate are his gifts. Wasteful are his Charities. He knows not the time or season or the person to whom gifts are to be made. His generosity is unwisdom. His Charities are error. Arjuna, are you listening ?

Arjuna (Sinking into trance) : With the most careful ears I listen.

Lord Krishna (Secretly pouring into Arjuna's ears the Sacred Word of the Vedic Rites) : Arjuna, then slumber.

Arjuna (Hearing with the inner ear the Sacred Words) : I hear a humming in my ears.

Lord Krishna : What do you hear ?

Arjuna : I cannot say.

Lord Krishna (Stimulating) : Try again.

Arjuna : I hear three sounds.

Lord Krishna : What is the first sound ?

Arjuna : AUM.

Lord Krishna : And the Second ?

Arjuna : TAT.

Lord Krishna : And the Third ?

Arjuna : SAT.

Lord Krishna (Explaining) : These are the three sounds of the Vedic Rites which purify Faith and the gifts of Faith.

Arjuna : What is the first sound ?

Lord Krishna : The Voice of the Creative Lord—AUM.

Arjuna : And the second ?

Lord Krishna : TAT signifying His Omnipresence.

Arjuna : And the third ?

Lord Krishna : SAT, the Omnipresent Reality.

Arjuna : What is the triple Word ?

Lord Krishna : I Brahma. I am AUM. I am TAT. I am SAT. I am the Paramatma.

Arjuna : What do the sacred syllables move to ?

Lord Krishna : To purification.

Arjuna : What do they purify ?

Lord Krishna : All Scriptures, all Rites, all Food, all Austerities, all Sacrifices, and all Faith.

Arjuna : Give me Lord the words of purification.

Lord Krishna : Your subtle ears have already heard the Vedic Sounds—

Arjuna : In my trance I have heard. I have heard !

Lord Krishna : Would you repeat the music ?

Arjuna : Yes.

Lord Krishna (Teaching the correct vowellation) : Follow My voice as it chants the chant of the ages. After Me slowly say : AUM.

Arjuna (Voicing) : AUM.

Lord Krishna : TAT.

Arjuna (Following the vowellation) : TAT.

Lord Krishna : SAT.

Arjuna (Musically chanting) : SAT.

Lord Krishna : Then repeat the triple word in one breath—the diapason of all sounds human or Divine.

Arjuna (Taking a long breath and uttering the sounds with inward power) : AUM, TAT, SAT.

Lord Krishna : Now Arjuna, rest.

Arjuna : I rest.

Lord Krishna : Arjuna I see you tomorrow ?

Arjuna (As Lord Krishna moves away) : May the morning sun see the end of the vast tear of Kurukshetra's field of sorrow.

Lord Krishna (Hinting coming events) : It will.

(*Exeunt Arjuna and Lord Krishna*).

SCENE XVIII

THE LAST RELEASE

(*On the seventeenth day of the battle, war on all fronts has ceased. The Armistice between the Kurus and the Pandavas has been signed. Arjuna and Lord Krishna are talking in the Chancellery awaiting the delegates of the Kurus who are about to deliver their note of the acceptance of the "Unconditional Surrender", when a courier knocks at the door of the Chancellery*).

Arjuna (Hearing a sound) : Who knocks ?

Courier : The courier.

Arjuna : What do you want ?

Courier : Immediate audience with your majesty.

Arjuna : Come in.

Courier (Entering) : Top-secret despatches for your Lordship.

Arjuna : Papers from the High Command ?

Courier : Yes.

Arjuna : Has the Armistice been signed ?

Courier : Yes, at dawn.

Arjuna : And the Cease-Fire ?

Courier : Cease-Fire has been proclaimed on all fronts.

Arjuna : Where has our armour halted ?

Courier : At the steps of the Chancellery.

Arjuna : Where are our armies ?

Courier : The armies of the Western and the Eastern Command have invested both gates of the Chancellery.

Arjuna : Where is the conjunction of our armies ?

Courier : At the Chancellery.

Arjuna : Now you may go. Report to us any fresh developments without delay.

Courier (Withdrawing) : I will my Lord.

Arjuna (To Lord Krishna) : My Lord shall we stroll about the ruins of the Chancellery ?

Lord Krishna : Yes.

Arjuna (Descending the steps) : What sulphur and what smoke !

What fire and what rubble ! Is this war or butchery ? Is this the triumph of peace ? Where is the victor or vanquished here ? Look, my Lord, there ! There our rocket dived deep nosing the soil for its victims. See, my Lord. There in the bunker of Duryodhana—

Courier (Dramatically returning) : Grave news my Lord.

Arjuna (Guessing) : Have the terms of the Cease-fire been broken by the Kurus ?

Courier : No.

Arjuna (Impatient) : What ails you man ? Speak up.

Courier (In tears) : My good Lord, Prince Duryodhana is dead !

Arjuna (Shocked) : Dead !

Courier : Yes, dead !

Arjuna : Where did he die ?

Courier : In the bunker of this Chancellery.

Arjuna : How did he die ?

Courier : The Prince shot himself—

Arjuna : Fearing the swift pursuit of our arms ?

Courier : I know not.

Arjuna : Where does his body lie ?

Courier : Burnt or stowed away, I cannot say.

Arjuna : Where is his entourage ?

Courier : Dead or escaped to the hills.

Arjuna : Where is his Minister of propaganda ?

Courier : Beside his late master in the bunker dead.

Arjuna : And his Air-Marshal ?

Courier : Under arrest in the cellars of the Chancellery.

Arjuna : Detain him there in lock and chains.

Courier : We have. He is under heavy guard.

Arjuna : Where is the chief of the Gestapo ?

Courier : Escaped in careful disguise ?

Arjuna : Arrest him as soon as you can.

Courier : I will.

Arjuna : And the Chief of Staffs of the Kurus ?

Courier : Some dead, some escaped, and the rest under arrest.

Arjuna : Maintain discipline in the city. No civilian population is to be oppressed. Pillage and violence will be severely punished. Transmit this directive to all the heads of our command.

Courier : I will.

Arjuna : Are all our generals in session ?

Courier : They all await you in the Chancellery.

Arjuna : Where are the delegates of the Kurus ?

Courier : Outside the doors of the Chancellery.

Arjuna : Announce to all hands that my Lord Krishna and I will attend to all business in the hall of the Chancellery.

Courier : I go my Lord.

Arjuna (Entering the central hall of the Chancellery) : My Lord Krishna, your seat (Pointing to the chair of the Presidium).

Lord Krishna (In session) : We begin. Call the delegates of the Kurus.

Courier : They are here my Lord.

Arjuna (Addressing the delegates) : What brings you here ?

Delegates : The term of the Armistice—

Arjuna : The terms of the Armistice have been abrogated by my directive this morning.

Delegates (Submitting) : What would you bid us do ?

Arjuna : Am I your counsellor today ?

Delegates : The concilium of Prince Duryodhana has been dissolved. Whom should we ask ?

Arjuna (Sternly) : Consult your conscience in this hour of peril. If our terms you negate, we withdraw the order of Cease-fire. Choose peace or war.

Delegates : We have chosen peace.

Arjuna : Then read this (Showing the paper of surrender).

Delegates : My Lord we have read the instrument of surrender.

Arjuna : Then sign here both the folios.

Delegates (Signing under pressure) : Here we sign it thus.

Arjuna : Signature is not enough. Do you understand what your pen signs ?

Delegates : Yes.

Arjuna (Testing) : Is the surrender conditional or unconditional ?

Delegates : Unconditional.

Arjuna (Noticing embarrassment) : What are you fingering ?

Delegates (Timorously) : We have in our hands the testament of Prince Duryodhana.

Arjuna : How is it pertinent to these negotiations ?

Delegates : Duryodhana has bequeathed all his public estate, gardens, and parks, to the Kurus—

Arjuna (Stiffly) : Are you seeking the abrogation of the terms of the surrender ?

Delegates : No.

Arjuna (Sternly) : Then understand that the will has no validity in our realms. The estates of Prince Duryodhana are forfeit to the Crown. The ample domains of the Kurus belong (pausing) to my Lord Krishna and me.

Delegates (Meekly) : We follow.

Arjuna : In my Lord Krishna's eyes and mine there are no Kurus and no Pandavas in our new dominions. I hereby proclaim to you and to all associates of our arms—our confederates and allies on the field of Kurukshetra—that all authority civil or military is now vested in me the sole sovereign of the House of the Pandavas counselled by my guide and master Lord Krishna.

Lord Krishna (Closing the ceremonies of surrender) : Now gentlemen go !

Delegates (Humbled) : We go as bidden.

Arjuna : Let the general staff also withdraw. We would be alone. (As everyone leaves) Thanks, gentlemen.

Lord Krishna : Let us move to words of peace from the words of war. What further points ?

Arjuna : What is the abandonment of works ? What is renunciation of works ? Their difference explain.

Lord Krishna : By abandonment is meant the abandonment of the fruits of work and not the cessation of work.

Arjuna : The man who has abandoned the fruits of work continues to work ?

Lord Krishna : Yes. How can work cease ?

Arjuna : Then what does he abandon ?

Lord Krishna : Desire.

Arjuna : And the work ?

Lord Krishna : The work moves to rarer planes of work by reason of the expulsion of the cravings.

Arjuna : What is renunciation of works ?

Lord Krishna : Cessation of work on the mental and physical planes—

Arjuna : With continuity of work on the spiritual planes of subtler densities ?

Lord Krishna : Yes.

Arjuna : Then work does not cease but is enlarged ?

Lord Krishna : Yes.

Arjuna : What is the distinction between abandonment and renunciation of works ?

Lord Krishna : In abandonment the motive for the work is abandoned and not the work itself. In renunciation the work itself is renounced.

Arjuna : What is the work of the renunciate of works ?

Lord Krishna : Work in rarer dimensions of the Spirit.

Arjuna : What happens to his work mental and physical in the kingdom of the corporeal ?

Lord Krishna : They cease partially or wholly.

Arjuna : The renunciate does not cease to act ?

Lord Krishna : Rather he acts in the wider ambits of the Atma.

Arjuna : Is all work evil ? Is all work to be renounced ?

Lord Krishna : Good work is not evil. Faith, Sacrifice, Austerities, Rites and Charities are not to be renounced—

Arjuna : Not even by the renunciate of Works ?

Lord Krishna : No. All good works are part of the works of the renunciate.

Arjuna : The renunciate does not renounce desireless works ?

Lord Krishna : No, he can work in different planes of action higher or lower simultaneously—

Arjuna : For the scope of his works is amplified by his renunciation ?

Lord Krishna : Yes.

Arjuna : What law governs the abandonment of the fruits of works ?

Lord Krishna : The law of the threefold Strands.

Arjuna : Sattwa, Rajas, and Tamas ?

Lord Krishna : Yes.

Arjuna : The works of Sattwa are pure ; the works of Rajas impure ; and the works of Tamas delusion ?

Lord Krishna : Yes.

Arjuna : What do the works of Sattwa evolve ?

Lord Krishna : The perfected Yogi.

Arjuna : And the works of Rajas ?

Lord Krishna : The man of desire.

Arjuna : And the works of Tamas ?

Lord Krishna : The man of sin.

Arjuna : To what do the works of Sattwa evolve ?

Lord Krishna : To the impersonal Self of the Atma.

Arjuna : And the works of Rajas ?

Lord Krishna : To the personal Self of matter.

Arjuna : And the works of Tamas ?

Lord Krishna : To the illusory Self of Maya.

Arjuna : What is the end of the works of Sattwa ?

Lord Krishna : Freedom from births.

Arjuna : And the end of the works of Rajas and Tamas ?

Lord Krishna : Rebirth in the fields of Samsara.

Arjuna : Where are the works of the Rajas and Tamas man ?

Lord Krishna : In the fields of delusion.

Arjuna : How are the works of delusion perfected ?

Lord Krishna : By the cycles of life in the fields of Maya.

Arjuna : How many are the causes of the cyclic life of Maya ?

Lord Krishna : Five.

Arjuna : What is the first cause ?

Lord Krishna : The Unmanifest.

Arjuna : What does the Unmanifest Manifest ?

Lord Krishna : The Not-Self and the fields of the Not-Self.

Arjuna : What is the second cause ?

Lord Krishna : The mind of the Not-Self.

Arjuna : What is the third cause ?

Lord Krishna : The mind and the five organs of perception cohering in the personality or Ego of man.

Arjuna : What is the fourth cause ?

Lord Krishna : The five organs of action.

Arjuna : What is the fifth cause ?

Lord Krishna : The invisible agencies of earth, air, and heaven which preside over the faculties of man.

Arjuna : These five causes are the root of all the actions of man ?

Lord Krishna : Yes.

Arjuna : All these causes of action proceed from the Not-Self ?

Lord Krishna : Yes.

Arjuna : And not from the Atma ?

Lord Krishna : No. For the Atma does not act.

Arjuna : What is Yogic release ?

Lord Krishna : Release from the five causes of the Not-Self which hold the soul in the fields of Samsara.

Arjuna : What happens when man is freed by the action of the Yogas ?

Lord Krishna : Man then knows that he is the instrument and not the doer of the action.

Arjuna : Whom does he know to be the doer of the action ?

Lord Krishna : Brahma.

Arjuna : Then he take no taint from any action ?

Lord Krishna : No.

Arjuna : Then when he kills, he does not kill ?

Lord Krishna : Yes.

Arjuna : Who kills or seems to kill ?

Lord Krishna : Brahma.

Arjuna : For killing is illusory ?

Lord Krishna : Yes.

Arjuna : What is the relationship between Knowledge and Action ?

Lord Krishna : Knowledge is the perception of the action to be done. The object of Knowledge is the action to be done. Knowledge is the means of action.

Arjuna : Then Knowledge and Action are necessary complementaries ?

Lord Krishna : Yes. For both are phases of the same action.

Arjuna : Knowledge and Action cannot be severed ?

Lord Krishna : No.

Arjuna : Who is the knower of the action ?

Lord Krishna : The Atma.

Arjuna : Who is not the knower of the action ?

Lord Krishna : The Not-Self—

Arjuna : For the Not-Self is Maya ?

Lord Krishna : Yes.

Arjuna : What is the Knowledge of the Sattwic man ?

Lord Krishna : The Knowledge that Brahma is the doer of all actions.

Arjuna : What is the Knowledge of the Rajas man ?

Lord Krishna : His Knowledge is Ignorance. He thinks he acts.

Arjuna : What is the Knowledge of the Tamas man ?

Lord Krishna : Maya. When he thinks he acts, he does not act.

Arjuna : Who is the master of his action ?

Lord Krishna : Brahma.

Arjuna : Where does the Sattwic man live ?

Lord Krishna : In the field of the One.

Arjuna : Where does the Rajas man live ?

Lord Krishna : In the field of the Many.

Arjuna : And the Tamas man ?

Lord Krishna : In no field at all.

Arjuna : What is the Knowledge of the Sattwic man ?

Lord Krishna : Truth.

Arjuna : And of the Rajas man ?

Lord Krishna : Guess.

Arjuna : And of the Tamas man ?

Lord Krishna : Delusion.

Arjuna : What is the action of the Sattwic man ?

Lord Krishna : Action free of attachments.

Arjuna : What is the action of the Rajas man ?

Lord Krishna : Action marred by desire.

Arjuna : What is the action of the Tamas man ?

Lord Krishna : Illusion.

Arjuna : What is the Sattwic man ?

Lord Krishna : The selfless doer of deeds for God.

Arjuna : What is the Rajas man ?

Lord Krishna : The selfish doer of deeds for himself.

Arjuna : What is the Tamas man ?

Lord Krishna : A wanderer on the roads of Samsara.

Arjuna : What does he do ?

Lord Krishna : Nothing. He is the deluded Ego imagining the deeds of a doer.

Arjuna : What is the reason of the Sattwic man ?

Lord Krishna : The illumined guidance of God.

Arjuna : What is the reason of the Rajas man ?

Lord Krishna : Reason spoiled by passion and therefore no reason.

Arjuna : What is the reason of the Tamas man ?
Lord Krishna : Reason destroyed by Maya and therefore unreason.
Arjuna : What is the constancy of the Sattwic man ?
Lord Krishna : The stability of restraint and virtue.
Arjuna : What is the constancy of the Rajas man ?
Lord Krishna : The pursuit of the desires.
Arjuna : What is the constancy of the Tamas man ?
Lord Krishna : The pursuit of sloth and lust.
Arjuna : What is the pleasure of the Sattwic man ?
Lord Krishna : The pleasure of the Sattwic man is veiled.
Arjuna : What is on the surface ?
Lord Krishna : Strife and suffering for the Good.
Arjuna : What is beneath the surface ?
Lord Krishna : Bliss.
Arjuna : God is Bliss ?
Lord Krishna : Yes.
Arjuna : Then the pleasure of the Sattwic man is God ?
Lord Krishna : Yes.
Arjuna : As there is nothing beyond God, his pleasure is absolute and complete ?
Lord Krishna : Yes.
Arjuna : What is the pleasure of the Rajas man ?
Lord Krishna : Passion.
Arjuna : Passion is pain ?
Lord Krishna : Yes.
Arjuna : Then the pleasure of the Rajas man is pain ?
Lord Krishna : Yes.
Arjuna : What is the pleasure of the Tamas man ?
Lord Krishna : Delusion.
Arjuna : What is delusive pleasure ?
Lord Krishna : Nothing.
Arjuna : Then the pleasure of the Tamas man is a void ?
Lord Krishna : Yes.
Arjuna : Are the three threads of the Not-Self Cosmic principles ?
Lord Krishna : The triple Strands are Cosmic Principles behind the mask of all actions.
Arjuna : Whom do they affect ?
Lord Krishna : All beings from man to angels.

Arjuna : What is the Sattwic Force ?

Lord Krishna : The concealed Force of the Spirit.

Arjuna : What is the Rajas Force ?

Lord Krishna : The restless Force of the Vital Soul.

Arjuna : Which is the Force of human Desire ?

Lord Krishna : Yes.

Arjuna : What is the Tamas Force ?

Lord Krishna : The Asuric Force of the Deluder.

Arjuna : Do the three Strands affect the fabric of human Society ?

Lord Krishna : Yes, they touch the four orders of Society—

Arjuna : The Brahmana Class ?

Lord Krishna : Yes.

Arjuna : What is the Brahmana Class ?

Lord Krishna : The Order of the Priesthood.

Arjuna : What is the Priesthood ?

Lord Krishna : The Hierarchy of the spiritual brotherhood in all creeds and religions in all Societies who practise Self-restraint, and purity of morals and clarities of mind with active deeds free of desire centred on My Light.

Arjuna : And the Ksatriya Class.

Lord Krishna : The Ksatriya Class is the order of My warriors in all Societies who by arms protect the civic liberties of My evolving orders.

Arjuna : And the Vaish Class ?

Lord Krishna : The Vaish Class is the order of My merchants who bring material prosperity to all Societies.

Arjuna : And the Sudra Class ?

Lord Krishna : The Sudra Class is the order of all My workers in all My Societies.

Arjuna : What order is higher and what lower ?

Lord Krishna : None. On the ascending ladder of Duty there is no Class.

Arjuna : Who makes the distinctions of the Classes ?

Lord Krishna : The lower mind of Maya.

Arjuna : All the Classes are one ?

Lord Krishna : Yes, because they proceed from the One.

Arjuna : Then your high Society is the Classless Society of Souls—

Lord Krishna : The Classless Society of all My workers who work for Me.

Arjuna : But each order has its functions due—

Lord Krishna : All duties are apportioned rank upon rank by My laws of Karma—

Arjuna : Which none else can do ?

Lord Krishna : Yes.

Arjuna : Then Classes are not Classes but gradations of work ?

Lord Krishna : Yes.

Arjuna : On the spiritual Ladder of Society merit moves to merit ?

Lord Krishna : Yes, by the just appointments of Karma.

Arjuna : What is on the last rung of the Ladder of Society ?

Lord Krishna : The order of My workers—the Sudra Class.

Arjuna : What is on the second rung ?

Lord Krishna : The order of My merchants—the Vaish Class.

Arjuna : What is on the third rung ?

Lord Krishna : The order of My warriors—the Ksatriya Class.

Arjuna : What is on the fourth rung ?

Lord Krishna : The order of My priests—the Brahmana Class.

Arjuna : What is the work on the last rung ?

Lord Krishna : The work of the Sudra Class in the fields of the Illusions—

Arjuna : Marked by the force of matter or Tamas ?

Lord Krishna : Yes.

Arjuna : What is the work on the second rung ?

Lord Krishna : The work of the Vaish Class in the fields of the cravings—

Arjuna : Marked by the vital force of desire ?

Lord Krishna : Yes.

Arjuna : What is the work on the third rung ?

Lord Krishna : The work of the Ksatriya Class in the field of War—

Arjuna : Marked by the vital force of the cravings—Rajas ?

Lord Krishna : Yes.

Arjuna : What is the work on the fourth rung ?

Lord Krishna : The work of the Brahmana Class in the field of the Spirit—

Arjuna : Marked by the spiritual force of Sattwa?

Lord Krishna : Yes.

Arjuna : Then the triple Strands of the Not-Self hold in bonds all the four orders of all the Societies of the earth?

Lord Krishna : Yes.

Arjuna : When will the Great Society arise?

Lord Krishna : When all Societies are freed from the three Strands of the Not-Self.

Arjuna : What shall be the new Society of the earth?

Lord Krishna : The Classless Society of Spirits.

Arjuna : For all your workers in different gradations of their duties are the Spirits of the Future Society?

Lord Krishna : Yes. All work is the labour of My Spirits. Therefore the Future Society must be the Society of My Spirits.

Arjuna : Each man then must to his function go—

Lord Krishna : The priest to the temple—

Arjuna : The warrior to battle—

Lord Krishna : The merchant to the mart—

Arjuna : The labourer to the field—

Lord Krishna : For all work is prayer and all work is I.

Arjuna : Who will collect the works of Man?

Lord Krishna : I am the Harvester of the works of all Societies. (Looking at Arjuna occultly) How goes it with you Arjuna?

Arjuna (Gazing back into Lord Krishna's eyes) : Well, my Lord.

Lord Krishna : Do you feel strange?

Arjuna : No.

Lord Krishna : Any touch of the Ray?

Arjuna (Unconscious of the occult operation) : No. Why do you speak so strangely Lord?

Lord Krishna : Soon will you understand the occult play of My eyes.

Arjuna : Are you playing with me Lord?

Lord Krishna : I am the play, the player, and the end of the play.

Arjuna (Not understanding) : What play?

Lord Krishna (Disclosing) : The play of Lord Krishna's eyes with the eyes of his disciple Prince Arjuna!

Arjuna (Realising the drama) : The play of Prince Arjuna's arms in Kurukshetra's holy field ?

Lord Krishna (Revealing) : Precisely !

Arjuna : Am I the pawn of Maya ?

Lord Krishna : Yes.

Arjuna : Are you the Lord of the stage of the illusions ?

Lord Krishna : Yes.

Arjuna : Am I the unconscious actor on the board of the illusions ?

Lord Krishna : Yes.

Arjuna : Is my work on Kurukshetra's meads the moving drama of the illusions ?

Lord Krishna : Yes.

Arjuna : Does the drama of Prince Arjuna and my Lord Krishna end ? Do the curtains fall ?

Lord Krishna : Not yet. Proceed with your last questions.

Arjuna (Under occult pressure) : My Lord, I feel strange as if in some higher range of Time I move !

Lord Krishna : Then ring out the changes. With broader lip extend the inquiries. Think of My Cosmic Whole and leave My Cosmic parts.

Arjuna (Boldly) : Tell me the whole range of the progression of the soul from matter to God.

Lord Krishna : In one sweep of Cosmic thought I shall speak. Interrogate !

Arjuna : How does the holy Monad to you climb ?

Lord Krishna : Through the many windows of the subtle illusions.

Arjuna : What does it see on the first windowsill ?

Lord Krishna : The false perception of the world of matter.

Arjuna : What lies beyond ?

Lord Krishna : The embodied soul bound in the sisterhood of the twin threads of Spirit and Matter.

Arjuna : And beyond ?

Lord Krishna : The Life Soul of the Universe dispossessed of Spirit and Matter.

Arjuna : And beyond ?

Lord Krishna : The Immaterial Soul the Jiva-Atma.

Arjuna : And beyond ?

Lord Krishna : The Atma or Oversoul.

Arjuna : And beyond?

Lord Krishna : The Paramatma or Absolute Spirit.

Arjuna : And beyond?

Lord Krishna : Beyond there is nothing.

Arjuna : What does the Monad see from the last window?

Lord Krishna : Three aspects of the Paramatma.

Arjuna : What does the Monad see as the First aspect of the Paramatma?

Lord Krishna : The neutral Brahma of imperishable glory without qualifications.

Arjuna : And how does it see the Second aspect?

Lord Krishna : As the Immutable Brahma with attributes.

Arjuna : How does it see the Third aspect?

Lord Krishna : As the manifold Brahma in divided unity in the field of the appearances.

Arjuna : How do the lids of the Monad open to the secret vision of the Paramatma?

Lord Krishna : By the roads of all My releases.

Arjuna : By the abandonment of the fruits of deeds?

Lord Krishna : Yes.

Arjuna : By cessation from work?

Lord Krishna : Yes.

Arjuna : By the Yoga of action?

Lord Krishna : Yes.

Arjuna : By the Yoga of mind?

Lord Krishna: Yes.

Arjuna : By the Yoga of Love?

Lord Krishna : Yes.

Arjuna (Summarising the teachings) : By all the Yogas in unity?

Lord Krishna : Yes.

Arjuna : By Karma Yog, Jnana Yog, Bhakti Yog, in combind efficacy of purpose?

Lord Krishna: Yes.

Arjuna : What is the last release?

Lord Krishna : I.

Arjuna : What are you Lord?

Lord Krishna : I am Hath Yoga. I am Karma Yoga. I am Jnana

Yoga. I am Bhakti Yoga. I am Shakti Yoga. I am Mantram Yoga. I am the Paramatma—

Arjuna : The seed, the source, the sum of all the releases ?

Lord Krishna : I am the grand release.

Arjuna : By what path should the lost soul lose you ?

Lord Krishna : By no path.

Arjuna : By what path should the lost soul find you ?

Lord Krishna : By one or all the paths. I am the release on every path—

Arjuna : You are my Lord the Watchman of the Highways—

Lord Krishna : Who will miss Me on the Cross-Roads ?

Arjuna : None.

Lord Krishna (Watching reactions) : Why so quiet Arjuna ?

Arjuna (With tears of love in his eyes) : What of your votary My Lord ?

Lord Krishna : No shadow stands on the Way you tread to Me.

Arjuna : For I have seen your Light on all the Ways—

Lord Krishna : And therefore by all the Ways you come to Me.

Arjuna : I understand.

Lord Krishna : Are now all your doubts ended ?

Arjuna : Yes.

Lord Krishna (Calling him by his occult eyes) : Prince !

Arjuna (Mystically responding) : Lord !

Lord Krishna (Drawing) : Creature !

Arjuna (Esoterically drawn) : Creator !

Lord Krishna (Esoterically embracing Arjuna) : In My holy bosom rest !

Arjuna (In supreme ecstasy) : I rest !

Lord Krishna (Pointing to the sunset) : Regard the West !

Arjuna : I do.

Lord Krishna (Speaking majestically) : From the smoke and flame of these ruined edifices, the awful spectacle and high hazard of war, embodying the imperial tear and agony of Man, Arjuna, with calm and disembodied eyes look upon yonder clouds of the sunset—

Arjuna : Whose flamboyant fleeces brighter than the bow of the Aurora Borealis incarnadine the sky—

Lord Krishna : As the fair lady of the Vesper with enflamed foot treads the empurpled air—

Arjuna : Ushering in the hastening strides of the twilight—

Lord Krishna : Whose bright flush drawn from the dying embers of the sinking sun silvers all the hills with evening's sheen—

Arjuna : At twilight, my Lord, the cooing dove returns to her nest—

Lord Krishna : At twilight the honeybee covered over with the lime and spoils of rose and thyme hushes her murmur in her clammy hive—

Arjuna : At twilight the glow-worm in the dewy grass trims her lantern for the night—

Lord Krishna : Are not dusk and twilight the fair names of all repose ?

Arjuna : So at twilight should not the hymn of the Bhagvad Gita close ?

Lord Krishna : Yes.

Arjuna : Close but to begin and begin but to close ?

Lord Krishna : Yes.

Arjuna : So let the Canticle of Canticles in the temple of the human heart for ever resound with the sound of the Word of God !

Lord Krishna : Happy dreams, dear Prince. Good night !

Arjuna : Sweet thoughts, Heavenly Sire ! Good night !

Lord Krishna (Leaving) : Good night, sweet Prince. Good night ! AUM.

(*At the sound of the mystic word AUM, the whole scene dissolves as a dream of Maya*).

EPILOGUE

"Beyond the great self is the unmanifest ! Beyond the unmanifest is the spirit. Beyond the spirit there is nothing. That is the end of the journey ! That is the final goal."

Katha Upanishad : Translated by Radhakrishnan.

(From a ring of radiance emerges a mystic Light without shape or form. In soft melodious accents it speaks the ABSTRACT PHILOSOPHY of the Gita).

Epilogue: I am the Epilogue. Long ago from Master Time had I parted. In my palms you see neither scythe nor sickle. I neither sow nor reap nor grow. I am not the beginning because I am beyond the end. I am not the Show because I am beyond the Show. As I am neither the beginning nor the end, I am the Beginningless and the Endless. I am in Time, out of Time, and beyond Time. I am the ABSTRACT PHILOSOPHY of the Gita. Try to know Me then. My name is the Full. Negate Me if you wish. Contemplate Me as the nought. Nought is nothing. Nothingness is the void. The void is the false. What is nought then ? The Full. Affirm Me if you can. Say: He is the Full. Affirmation cannot encompass Me. The Full beyond all lips doth flee. Try again to lisp My elusive Name. Take the Full from the Full. What remains ? The Full. Add the Full to the Full. What abides? The Full. Multiply the Full. What is the sediment, what the increment ? The Full. Addition, Subtraction, Multiplication, or Division, cannot change the nature of the Full. How then will you seize the Full ? By the Yoga of the Full? What is the Yoga of the Full? (Looking at the book of the Bhagvad Gita in his hands materialised). My Lords, here is the Full. Look at Lord Krishna in your heart. My noble Lords, look at this BOOK ! AUM. TAT. SAT.

(*Upon the recital of the sacred words of the Gita, the mystic Light vanishes*).